William Shakespeare

Hamlet

Ann Thompson
&
Neil Taylor

Northcote House

in association with
The British Council

For Philip Edwards
an editor of *Hamlet* who was
not seduced by Hamlet

© Copyright 1996 by Ann Thompson & Neil Taylor

First published in 1996 by Northcote House Publishers Ltd, Plymbridge House, Estover Road, Plymouth PL6 7PZ, United Kingdom. Tel: (01752) 735251. Fax: (01752) 695699.

British Library Cataloguing-in-Publication Data
A catalogue record for this book is available from the British Library

ISBN 0 7463 0765 9

Typeset by Kestrel Data, Exeter
Printed and bound in the United Kingdom by BPC Wheatons Ltd, Exeter

ISOBEL ARMSTRONG
General Editor

BRYAN LOUGHREY
Advisory Editor

University of CHESTER CAMPUS
Chester LIBRARY
01244 513301

This book is to be returned on or before the last date stamped below. Overdue charges will be incurred by the late return of books.

HAMLET AND HORATIO WITH THE GRAVEDIGGERS
from a lithograph by EUGÈNE DELACROIX *of 1843*
Copyright British Museum

Contents

Illustrations

Acknowledgements

We are currently preparing an edition of *Hamlet* for the Arden Shakespeare (third series) and we have appreciated the opportunity to work on this book simultaneously. We have presented some of our ideas to colleagues at conferences in Stratford-upon-Avon and New York, and when giving papers in London, Oxford, and Barcelona; we are grateful for the feedback received on those occasions. We also owe a considerable debt to Sasha Roberts for her help in bibliographical research, and to Pauline Kiernan for her research on stage history. John O. Thompson kindly read and commented on the penultimate version of the typescript.

Illustration Acknowledgements

The Authors and the Publishers gratefully acknowledge the following for supplying illustrations and granting permission for their use.

British Film Institute, London (Plate 5); British Museum, London (Cover detail, Frontispiece, Plate 3); the Raymond Mander and Joe Mitchenson Theatre Collection, London (Plate 7); the Royal Library, Copenhagen (Plate 4; catalogue signature: Thott 797 fol.); Stuart Morris, photographer (Plate 8); the Tate Gallery, London (Plate 2); the Trustees of the Victoria and Albert Museum, London (Plates 1 and 6).

References and Dates

Quotations from *Hamlet* and from all other works by Shakespeare are taken from *The Riverside Shakespeare* edited by G. Blakemore Evans (Boston, 1974). Dates of Shakespeare's works are based on those given in 'The Canon and Chronology of Shakespeare's Plays' in *William Shakespeare: A Textual Companion* by Stanley Wells and Gary Taylor with John Jowett and William Montgomery (Oxford, 1987), pp. 69–144.

1

Shakespeare's Greatest Play?

I suspect that for the immediate future *King Lear* will continue to be regarded as the central achievement of Shakespeare, if only because it speaks more largely than the other tragedies to the anxieties and problems of the modern world. (R. A. Foakes, *'Hamlet' versus 'Lear'*, 1993, p. 224)

Nothing can be taken for granted, not even the primacy of *King Lear*. We may be returning to the *Hamlet* mood that dominated the nineteenth century. (Maurice Charney, *'Bad' Shakespeare*, 1988, p. 14)

Is *Hamlet* still Shakespeare's greatest play? Some 400 years after it was written, the jury is apparently still out. Or perhaps one should say that the verdict is being challenged by a late appeal. As R. A. Foakes demonstrates in his recent book, *'Hamlet' versus 'Lear'*, an unprecedented shift took place in the canonical status of *Hamlet* between 1955 and 1965. Before 1955 it was generally regarded as the greatest of Shakespeare's tragedies, but during the following decade it was displaced by *King Lear* which was at the same time being reinterpreted not as a redemptive parable but as a bleak vision of suffering and despair. Without claiming a direct connection between the reception of Shakespeare's plays and the political events of the time, Foakes nevertheless sees at least a coincidence between the new assessment of *King Lear* and the mood of the Cold War period with its threat of total devastation caused by the world's growing nuclear arsenals; the grim exchange between Kent and Edgar – 'Is this the promis'd end? | Or image of that horror?' (V. iii. 264–5) – took on a topical level of meaning. For a time too, that play seemed to offer a mirror

1

of a late-twentieth-century world controlled by old men obsessed with power, though the relevance of this analogy has happily weakened with the decline of the former Soviet Union and its satellite regimes in Eastern Europe (not to mention the retirement of Ronald Reagan in the USA). By the same token, however, one might wonder at the apparent lack of appeal of *Hamlet*, on one level a tragedy of youth, and dissident youth at that, to the generation of the late 1960s and early 1970s, a period now seen nostalgically as a golden age of radicalism and rebellion.

Is Foakes right to assume that the relatively recent re-evaluation of these plays will hold, or will future generations look back on the current supremacy of *King Lear* as a curious aberration in the otherwise unquestioned sway of *Hamlet* as 'top play' as our quotation from Maurice Charney implies? How does such a literary league table operate and does it really matter anyway? In this section we shall address these questions which do seem unavoidable when one is considering a cultural work of such a formidable status as *Hamlet*.

To begin with, we are not just talking about private aesthetic judgements made by literary critics. The status of a Shakespearean play is directly reflected in such things as the number and scale of performances it is given (will it for example fill a big theatre or can it only be risked in a studio space?), the number of copies of the text sold, and the frequency with which it is prescribed as a 'set text' in school, college, and university syllabuses. It is also evident more intangibly in the ways in which it is seen to 'speak to us' as measured by the level and intensity of critical debate, and the extent to which the play inspires modern writers to adapt it and allude to it in their own work. *King Lear* has certainly scored highly on this last scale recently with 'offshoots' to works ranging from Edward Bond's play *Lear* (1971) to Jane Smiley's novel *A Thousand Acres* (1991). Another play which clearly strikes a twentieth-century topical chord is *The Tempest*, which has been a source for a number of colonial and post-colonial adaptations including Suniti Namjoshi's sequence of poems *Snapshots of Caliban* (1984) and Marina Warner's novel *Indigo* (1992). *Hamlet* has apparently been less seminal in this respect since Akira Kurosawa's film *The Bad Sleep Well* (1960) and Tom Stoppard's play *Rosencrantz and Guildenstern are Dead* (1966). It may also be significant that while Kurosawa takes on the central themes of paternity and revenge, Stoppard re-presents the story from the point of view of the ignorant and confused courtiers as a tragicomedy of alienation and absurdity in the mode of Samuel Beckett.

It is difficult to imagine history differently, but from the perspective of 1600 it might have seemed unlikely that *Hamlet* should ever have achieved its high level of canonical status in the first place. It is after all the earliest of what we have come to see as the 'big four' texts since A. C. Bradley's influential *Shakespearean Tragedy* (1904) which elevated it above the other plays, along with *Othello* (1603–4), *King Lear* (1605) and *Macbeth* (1606). It was written at a point when Shakespeare's previous experience of writing tragedy consisted of *Titus Andronicus* (1592), *Romeo and Juliet* (1594–5) and *Julius Caesar* (1599). *Titus Andronicus* and *Romeo and Juliet* look in retrospect like precocious, in some ways brilliant, one-off experiments with modes of tragedy Shakespeare chose not to pursue, while *Julius Caesar* is usually discussed today as a 'Roman play' rather than as a tragedy. Nevertheless, it seems important to consider *Hamlet* from this perspective, as well as alongside the later plays.

Hamlet does have links with all three of its generic predecessors. As we shall see in chapter 4, it shares a rhetorical self-consciousness with *Titus Andronicus* and *Romeo and Juliet*, and all three of these early tragedies are to a greater or lesser extent built around the interlocking revenge feuds of two powerful families. They all have climactic scenes which focus on a tomb or graveyard. There seems to be a self-conscious allusion to Shakespeare's own *Julius Caesar* in *Hamlet* when Polonius tells Hamlet about his experience of acting at university:

I did enact Julius Caesar. I was kill'd i'th'Capitol; Brutus kill'd me.

(III. ii. 103–4)

Members of the original audience might have been aware that the actor of Polonius (probably John Heminges) had indeed recently appeared at the Globe as Caesar and (ominously) that the actor playing Hamlet (Richard Burbage) had appeared as Brutus.

More substantially, both Brutus and Hamlet are represented as intellectual, sensitive men who are required to become murderers (and murderers of father-figures) somewhat against their temperaments and better judgements. The nature of the task is suggested in *Julius Caesar* but examined in *Hamlet*. When Brutus is contemplating the murder of Caesar he says:

> Since Cassius first did whet me against Caesar,
> I have not slept.
> Between the acting of a dreadful thing
> And the first motion, all the interim is
> Like a phantasma or a hideous dream.
> The Genius and the mortal instruments
> Are then in council; and the state of man,
> Like to a little kingdom, suffers then
> The nature of an insurrection.

(II. i. 61–9)

The 'interim' between the 'first motion' (suggestion, awareness of an obligation to kill) and 'the acting of a dreadful thing' (the killing itself) along with the accompanying 'insurrection' in the microcosm is what Shakespeare actually explores in the experience of Hamlet, not Brutus. And he looks back in the later play to the ominous eruption of the supernatural as part of the 'hideous dream' in *Julius Caesar*. In his attempt to explain the appearance of the Ghost at the beginning of *Hamlet* Horatio draws a parallel for his listeners:

> In the most high and palmy state of Rome,
> A little ere the mightiest Julius fell,
> The graves stood tenantless and the sheeted dead
> Did squeak and gibber in the Roman streets.

(I. i. 113–16)

The Ghost in *Hamlet* is more concerned with the past than with the future, but neither Brutus nor Hamlet succeeds in purifying the state of the corruption they perceive in it and which they aim to eliminate by violent action.

Canonical status is allied to genre, and tragedy has always had a higher and more canonical status than comedy or history, but *Hamlet* was for a time threatened with losing that status when it was classified earlier in the twentieth century by E. M. W. Tillyard and others as a 'problem play' (1950), allied to a group of texts Shakespeare wrote around the turn of the century – *Troilus and Cressida, Measure for Measure* and *All's Well That Ends Well* – which were all seen as being characterized by a mood of philosophical abstraction and speculation, as well as by an obsession with the 'darker' aspects of sexuality, and hence 'problematic' in the same way as the more recent plays of Ibsen and Strindberg. Unlike the other works involved, *Hamlet* did not languish for long in the 'problem play' category, but it may have been demoted more insidiously by some of the ways in which its particular kind of tragedy has been analysed. John Dover Wilson's *What Happens in 'Hamlet'* (1935) implicitly limited the play's appeal by attempting to recover its Elizabethan nature and the likely response of its original audience. Similarly, Fredson Bowers' study of *Elizabethan Revenge Tragedy* (1940) and Eleanor Prosser's *Hamlet and Revenge* (1967), while illuminating many aspects of the play, set it in a relatively remote historical and literary context by putting stress on such things as the ethics of revenge and the Elizabethan belief in ghosts. Thus *Hamlet* may have begun to seem in the mid-twentieth century primitive and quaint, an appropriate subject for academic and antiquarian investigation but not very relevant to the modern world, while at the same time *King Lear* had suddenly become topical.

A further possible threat to the canonical status of *Hamlet*, and one which also affects *King Lear*, is the extent to which both plays have been problematized by the debates which have taken place in the last fifteen years over the origins and status of the variant early printed texts and the relations between them. Up until about 1980, all claims that either play was Shakespeare's greatest tragedy were based on the kind of 'conflated' texts which we are now encouraged to reject as inauthentic constructions of interfering editors. We shall discuss some of the relevant issues in more detail in chapter 2, but they do impinge upon arguments about the relative merits of the plays in so far as editors and critics now find themselves disagreeing over which *text* of *Hamlet* or *Lear* is better or more authoritative. It is becoming extremely difficult to discuss either play without grasping a very complex set of textual

5

issues, and one sometimes feels that the impact of the plays themselves is in danger of being dissipated by an over-attention to variant readings.

Nevertheless, *Hamlet* remains in at least two important ways more powerful as a cultural icon within English drama than *King Lear*: it is generally considered to be a significant milestone in the career of the aspiring actor, and it is instantly recognizable as an allusion or reference point by a number of well-known moments or images.

The role of Hamlet is still seen as one of the major challenges facing an actor, an initiation test or a mountain he has to climb in order to prove his skill and commitment to his career. As we show in chapter 5, it has even been regarded as reasonable that women should also take it on, partly because it is simply one of the best roles the stage has to offer. The role of King Lear has not yet acquired anything like the same status, perhaps because of that play's far more limited and perverse stage history. *Hamlet* has an unusual record of virtually continual performance with minimal adaptation, even during the Restoration and eighteenth century when most of Shakespeare's plays were radically re-written. It is notorious however that Shakespeare's version of *King Lear* was not performed at all for about 150 years after 1681, during which time Nahum Tate's adaptation with its happy ending was generally preferred. Now that *Lear* is finally seen as not un-stageable, it may be that the title-role as well as the play will take on a more canonical status. But if it does, it will surely be regarded rather differently: as an older man's part it will be the culmination of an already successful career, while Hamlet remains the role in which a young (or younger middle-aged) actor can make his mark as a 'star' comparatively early on.

Now, more than before, Hamlet has to be tackled early. Since the rise of the cinema in the twentieth century and the accompanying insistence on naturalistic casting – at least as far as age is concerned – it is now unthinkable that an actor could play Hamlet on stage at the age of 74 as Thomas Betterton did in 1709, or on screen at the age of 60 as Johnston Forbes-Robertson did in 1913. It is also more difficult to cast against body-type, as witness the pudgy Simon Russell Beale's apparent ineligibility for the role, despite both his own expressed desire to play it and Gertrude's famous remark that Hamlet is 'fat' (V. ii. 287). Recent film versions starring women, for example the Canadian film with Caroline Johnson directed by René Bonnière in 1971, are obscure curiosities, not the internationally applauded sensation achieved by Asta Nielsen in 1920 (see Plate 5).

The continuing significance of the role can be seen in two recent examples, Daniel Day-Lewis on stage (directed by Richard Eyre at the National Theatre, London, 1989) and Mel Gibson on screen (directed by Franco Zeffirelli in an American production, 1990). Both actors came to the role with a considerable performance record already behind them, but the Anglo-Irish Day-Lewis seemed the more likely casting, with his experience on the English stage as well as on screen in 'heritage' films such as James Ivory's adaptation of E. M. Forster's *A Room With A View*. The Australian Gibson was best known for his roles in science-fiction action films (notably the *Mad Max* series) and lacked the classical training Day-Lewis had acquired at the Bristol Old Vic. In the event, however, the critical consensus, to the surprise of some of the critics themselves, was that Gibson succeeded in the role where Day-Lewis failed.

And *Hamlet* remains the more instantly recognizable point of reference, a kind of cultural touchstone or talisman that is the source of more quotations and allusions than *King Lear* has yet generated. Again, the latter's supposed unstageability may be partly to blame; there is just not the backlog of images and illustrations available. One suspects that few if any lines from *Lear* would be readily identified by the average person on the streets of London or New York, while 'To be or not to be' must be the most familiar and frequently quoted (and parodied) speech in the western dramatic tradition, appearing for example in such a wide range of cinematic texts as John Ford's Western *My Darling Clementine* (1946), Frank Launder's *The Pure Hell of St Trinians* (1960) where it accompanies a strip-tease, and Woody Allen's *Everything You Always Wanted to Know About Sex, But Were Afraid To Ask* (1972). Not to mention the two films actually called *To Be Or Not To Be* (the 1942 original starring Jack Benny and directed by Ernst Lubitsch, and the 1983 remake, starring Mel Brooks and directed by Alan Johnson).

Other specific moments in the play appear over and over again as visual allusions in all kinds of contexts, serious, burlesque or banal. We can recognize at once the appearance of the Ghost on the battlements (a popular cover-illustration for paperback editions), the play-scene with Hamlet's attention fixed on the guilty King, the drowning of Ophelia (see Plates 1–3). The most familiar of all is the man holding a skull: such an image immediately evokes Hamlet's stance in the graveyard and the line 'Alas, poor Yorick!' (V. i. 184). *King Lear* does not (yet) have the equivalent of 'To be or not to be'; nor does it have such a set of instantly recognizable visual images. The most frequently depicted moments from the play (at least in the tradition of classical painting, as exemplified for example by the collections of the Royal Shakespeare Company in Stratford and the Folger Shakespeare Library in Washington, DC) are the opening scene with Lear dividing up his kingdom, represented by a map, and the final scene with Lear's entry carrying his dead daughter Cordelia. Even these would probably not instantly signify '*Lear*' to most people in the same way that the man with the skull signifies '*Hamlet*'. In this respect at least, *Hamlet* has not yet been displaced.

2

Which *Hamlet?*

A story of Hamlet is very old. In Denmark and Iceland, the exploits of the clever son whose name means 'stupid' (Amlodi, Amblett (see Plate 4) or Amleth) were being narrated at least 600 years before Shakespeare composed his play about the intellectual who adopts an antic disposition. But there is also a wider and older network of stories about sons who avenge their fathers' deaths – not just the northern legends of Havelok the Dane, King Horn and Bevis of Hampton, but the Persian legend of Kei Chosra and the Greek legend of Orestes. Shakespeare knew well at least one in this network, the story of Lucius Junius Brutus, who supposedly founded the Roman republic in 509 BC, who is the central character in Shakespeare's poem of *The Rape of Lucrece* and a potent allusion in his play of *Julius Caesar*, and whose name Brutus also means 'stupid'.

These were clearly ancient folk-tales with their own oral history before they got written down. Saxo Grammaticus recorded the Nordic story of Hamlet in about AD 1200 in his Latin collection of tales first printed in Paris in 1514, the *Gesta Danorum*. We do not know how Shakespeare came by the story, but it may have been via one or both of two routes. He may possibly have read it in volume 5 of François de Belleforest's popular collection of *Histoires Tragiques*, first published in French in 1570. It did not appear in English until 1608, by which time Shakespeare's play was already written, performed, and published. It is more likely that he knew of the story via a play about Hamlet (referred to by scholars as the *Ur-Hamlet*) which seems to have been seen on the London stage in or before 1589.

Shakespeare's *Hamlet* is therefore probably a revision of a dramatic treatment of a retelling of a literary treatment of a Scandinavian legend.

In Saxo's version of the legend there is no Laertes, no mad songs and suicide for his sister, no Osric, no gravediggers, no players and no play, but one can nevertheless find equivalents of almost all the figures who are essential to Shakespeare's plot – Old Hamlet and Young Hamlet, Old Fortinbras and Young Fortinbras, Claudius, Gertrude, Polonius, Horatio, Ophelia, Rosencrantz and Guildenstern, and the King of England. Furthermore, the legend has six plot-elements, all of which appear in Shakespeare's play:

(1) The villain kills his brother, the King. He thereby inherits the throne and marries his sister-in-law, the Queen.

(2) The hero, the late King's clever son (an inveterate punster and riddler), protects himself from his uncle and provides a cover for his revenge by pretending to be an idiot.

(3) The villain suspects the hero is not stupid and tempts him to seduce an attractive young woman; but the hero makes it seem that he has resisted the temptation.

(4) The villain tests the hero a second time, by planting a spy in the Queen's bedroom to overhear her talking to her son; but the spy is discovered by the hero and killed.

(5) The villain tests the hero a third time, by sending him to a foreign country with two escorts, who carry instructions to the foreign king to have him killed; but the hero outwits them and arranges for them to be killed instead.

(6) The hero arrives home during a funeral, kills the villain after an exchange of swords, and becomes king.

The one essential plot element which does not persist into Belleforest and Shakespeare is the ending of the story. Shakespeare's Hamlet dies as he becomes king, but Saxo's Amleth lives on to experience many further adventures, including the acquisition of a second wife (he has already married the Princess of England, and now he marries the Queen of Scotland).

But this is not to say that the later adventures are irrelevant to the study of *Hamlet*. For what they record are incidents which display more of Amleth's cunning and intelligence, and his concern with the telling of his own story. He has it engraved on his shield, and it is because the Queen of Scotland can 'read' that story in his shield that she decides not to kill him but to marry him instead. As Shakespeare's Hamlet lies dying he is keen that Horatio should report his cause aright (V. ii. 339).

The later incidents also provide further examples of that idea which so dominates Hamlet's mind – the moral frailty of women. Herminthrud, the Scottish Queen, whom Amleth is sent to woo on behalf of the King of Britain, always has her suitors murdered. Amleth nevertheless weds her, but after his death she weds his killer. Saxo comments: 'All vows of women become void with changes of fortune, are dissolved by the shifting of time, and disappear with the play of fate, for their faith stands on slippery feet. Though they are quick to promise you something, they are slow to keep it. Slaves of pleasure, they leap headfirst and gaping in their continual longing for something new, and forget the old' (William F. Hansen's translation, in his *Saxo Grammaticus and the Life of Hamlet*, 1983, p. 117).

The treachery of women may possibly be emblematized much earlier in the story: Amleth survives his first test with the young woman (3) because he is warned by his foster-brother, who sends him a gadfly with a straw embedded in its back. This is not easy to interpret, but at least one scholar, Geoffrey Bullough, proposed that the message was that Amleth should beware of 'the sting in the woman's tail' (*Narrative and Dramatic Sources of Shakespeare*, vol.7, p. 12, n.1). Of course, it may be that the truer misogynist was not Saxo, but Bullough.

In many respects, Shakespeare's play differs from the legend he takes over. While each of the first three elements is present in both Saxo and Shakespeare, there are variations in their treatments of them – and these variations often introduce ambiguities and problems of interpretation.

For example, in Saxo it is no secret that the villain has murdered the King (1). In Shakespeare, no one knows – unless Gertrude does, but there is no sound reason to believe she does – so Hamlet has to be told and, following Belleforest, Shakespeare introduces a ghost to tell him. In Saxo, because the crime is public knowledge, the hero needs the disguise of idiocy lest his uncle suspect he is up to something (2). In Shakespeare, the villain has no reason to believe that Hamlet knows anything, so the antic disposition is unnecessary – but may reveal something about Hamlet's inner state of mind. In Saxo, the hero realizes that he is being seduced into seducing the girl (3). In Shakespeare it is unclear whether or not Hamlet knows that Ophelia is being used to make him reveal his secrets.

On the other hand, sometimes the differences between Saxo and Shakespeare are not as great as they appear. It seems on the surface that Shakespeare has rejected that part of element 4 of the Saxo story where, having killed the spy in his mother's bedchamber, Amleth cuts him up and feeds him to the pigs. But in fact Hamlet has as little respect for Polonius's corpse, deciding to 'lug the guts' next door (III. iv. 212) and then telling the King that, just as his councillor has become a diet of worms, so he will one day be making a royal progress through the guts of a beggar (IV. iii. 16–31).

More interesting is what happens to the funeral (6). In Saxo it is a false funeral, because the villain has organized it for the hero (believing he will have been killed in England) and the hero proves not to be dead at all. In Shakespeare it is a real ceremony for someone who is really dead, Ophelia. Yet there are two respects in which Shakespeare has retained an aspect of Saxo's treatment. In the first place, Laertes protests that there is something less than genuine about this funeral too. And this is because Ophelia's death was suspected suicide, so that the priest is unhappy about staging a ceremony at all. Secondly, there is an ironical sense in which, as in Saxo, it *is* the hero's funeral. Not only does it seal Hamlet's death warrant, because he declares his presence and thereby informs Claudius that he has outwitted him and survived the plot to have him killed by the King of England – in addition, Hamlet symbolizes that fact by leaping into the grave as if he were claiming it for himself.

Then again, in Saxo, Amleth carefully plans his revenge and achieves it by deliberately burning down the villain's hall while his retainers are inebriated in the funeral celebrations. In Shakespeare, Hamlet has no straightforward revenge-strategy, and the deaths of Claudius, Gertrude, and Laertes come about almost by accident. But it is possible that Shakespeare's Hamlet has a deeper strategy, incomplete and stumbling, perhaps, but in its roundabout way – as Polonius puts it, 'we . . . By indirections find directions out' (II. i. 61–3) – working towards the equivalent of Amleth's firing of the hall. In order to catch, not the life, but the *conscience* of the King, Hamlet stages a play in Claudius's castle, and the outcome is that the King is 'frighted with false fire' (III. ii. 266).

The effect of these changes to the story is that a new range of possible meanings is generated. Those meanings exist ultimately in the minds of readers and audiences, and are determined in part by the cultural conditions under which the play is being read or performed. The emergence of the novel in the late eighteenth century and its development as a site of realist character-study in the nineteenth century encouraged a reading of *Hamlet* which emphasized Shakespeare's apparent achievement in creating a complex individual who would repay psychological analysis in depth. Thus A. C. Bradley found himself inventing new elements in the story in order to explain what he felt to be realist problems in the portrayal of Hamlet, and engaging in discussions about the essential nature of other characters (such as Gertrude) based on an analysis of their behaviour as if he knew them intimately. In exactly the same way, twentieth-century psychoanalytic readings, such as those by Sigmund Freud, Ernest Jones, and Jacques Lacan, involve the claim to know something about Hamlet's childhood and unconscious. The reader is engaged in writing a longer and more detailed version of the Hamlet story than even Shakespeare produced.

Each of the issues referred to in the preceding section – the effect on Hamlet of his encounter with the Ghost, the ambiguity in Hamlet's adoption of an antic disposition, the ambiguity in his behaviour towards Ophelia, the significance of his seemingly unfeeling response to the death of Polonius, the interest in suicide, and the sense in which Hamlet is an unconventional revenger, motivated by unusual ambitions and needs – arises from features in Shakespeare's distinctive development of the story he took over. And few students of the play in the last 200 years have wished to resist the temptation to discuss these issues in anything other than realist terms, attempting to plumb what are perceived as the depths of Hamlet's character and mind.

A most prominent feature of Shakespeare's treatment is the extent of his use of the long soliloquy: this emphasis on the presentation of a character's inner life not only marks his treatment out from earlier versions of the story, it marks *Hamlet* out from most other plays written before or since. T. S. Eliot argued that, if he was going to write about the kind of mind revealed by the combination of Hamlet's actions and Hamlet's soliloquies, Shakespeare chose the wrong story to do it through. There is a mismatch between the play Shakespeare was trying to write and the play he ended up writing, and that imperfect fit arises from his inability to develop the Hamlet story enough to deliver the emotional material he is trying to deal with. (There is surely a logical problem here. If the play does indeed fail to communicate certain emotions, it is hard to think how Eliot was in a position to know what those emotions were!)

A hundred or so years earlier Goethe and Hegel were also struggling with Hamlet's inner life. For them, Hamlet was too sensitive a soul. It was not that Hamlet was unsuited to *Hamlet*, he was unsuited to this world at all, because he was such a delicate and tender prince – as, ironically, Hamlet describes Fortinbras. Others, including Fortinbras himself, have argued that, other things being equal, Hamlet was perfectly suited to this world. He would have made an excellent King of Denmark but, unfortunately, by the time he drops out of his course of study at the University of Wittenberg, he has failed to learn enough about how to be a successful Revenge Hero.

It is sometimes said that Hamlet is a successful student of life, learning how to live as he learns how to die. This means that Shakespeare has created a character who develops. The Hamlet at the beginning of the play is deep in an inexplicable adolescent gloom and bitterness. The Hamlet liberated by the idea that he is justified in his feeling of hatred and contempt for his stepfather and moral anger at his mother becomes bloodthirsty in imagination but ineffectual in his pretensions to action. The Hamlet who kills Polonius believing him to be the King and then confronts his mother with his criticisms of her conduct is thereby relieved of a burden and free to pursue his revenge. But the opportunity is suddenly removed as he is himself removed from Denmark. On his return he is calmer, fatalistic and ready to seize opportunity by the forelock if she ever presents it fleetingly to him. This is a man, we are told, who has grown up before our eyes. When he says 'There's a divinity that shapes our ends, | Rough-hew them how we will' (V. ii. 10) he seems to be articulating a profound and useful fatalism he has learnt through the experience of the play up to the moment when he returns to Denmark. And that fatalism is a religious, even Christian, belief that the universe provides the son grieving over the loss of a father with another father-figure. When he tells Horatio that he believes 'There is special providence in the fall of a sparrow' (V. ii. 219–20), he seems to be alluding to Christ's words in Matthew 10:29, 'Are not two sparrows sold for a farthing? and one of them shall not fall on the ground without your Father'.

But it could equally be argued that Hamlet learns nothing – certainly nothing at all Christian – from his experience. In Act I he is contemplating suicide (ii. 129–320); in Act III most people think he is still contemplating suicide when he says 'To be or not to be, that is the question' (ii. 57); in Act V many actors playing Hamlet have him commit suicide by drinking poison on the line 'Give me the cup. Let go! By heaven, I'll ha't!' (ii. 343). In Act III he kills Laertes' father (iv. 24); in Act V he tries to disown responsibility for the act (ii. 230–2). Between scenes iv and vi of Act IV he arranges the deaths of his school-friends; in Act V he tells Horatio that he found 'heaven ordinant' when he dispatched them (ii. 48) and, furthermore, 'They are not near my conscience' (ii. 58).

The plot as Shakespeare has devised it is an insistent, multiple action, returning again and again to narratives of the deaths of kings and fathers and the carrying out of revenge by their sons. Hamlet is required by his father's ghost to 'Revenge his foul and most unnatural murther' (I. v. 25) and goes on to kill the murderer. In the next Act he asks the Player to recite a description of Pyrrhus avenging the death of his father, Achilles (II. ii. 465). A further Act on (III. ii. 103–4) Polonius recalls playing Julius Caesar and being killed in the Capitol by Brutus (a murder avenged in history – and in Shakespeare's own recently performed play – by Caesar's reputed son, Mark Antony). Hamlet then (III. ii. 135–270) arranges for a performance of a play, *The Murder of Gonzago*, in which he and the King see a parallel with the murder of Old Hamlet. In the last Act, Hamlet is challenged to a duel with Laertes and he confesses, 'by the image of my cause I see | The portraiture of his' (V. ii. 77–8). Finally, Fortinbras achieves revenge for the death of his father at the hands of Old Hamlet, when he walks into the Danish court to discover that the whole Hamlet family is dead (V. ii. 362).

15

Before Fortinbras completes his revenge both Laertes and Hamlet have completed theirs. But each achieves it in his own way. Fortinbras finds it absurdly easy, while Hamlet finds it absurdly difficult. Indeed, when Hamlet begins his quest his priority is not so much revenge, or justice, or punishment, as a kind of spiritual mission: not to kill Claudius but to confront him publicly with his state of sin, to reveal him to the world as a guilty creature. And that sin is as much a matter of his adultery as of his fratricide. Hamlet has a revenge aesthetic, he seeks the symmetry of an eye for an eye – it is not enough for Claudius to die, but he must experience a degree of suffering which will hold the mirror up to Old Hamlet's suffering and that suffering must occur in a context which is apt. Thus he can kill him in Gertrude's closet (unfortunately, his victim turns out to be Polonius) but he cannot kill him at prayer when he may have purged his sin.

In the same way, Hamlet wants to confront his mother with her state of sin, force her to reveal publicly (by blushing) her 'shame' at her 'trespass' (III. iv. 81, 146); then, however, in contrast with his strategy for his uncle, he wants to save her soul, by making her 'Confess' and 'Repent' (III. iv. 149, 150). But what is the play saying about revenge? It was written in an officially Christian country, it has a Christian setting (Marcellus calls Jesus 'our Saviour' I. i. 159) and the Christian Church preaches forgiveness, not revenge (in Shakespeare's *The Tempest* Prospero asserts that 'The rarer action is | In virtue than in vengeance', V. i. 27–8). Because there's a divinity that shapes our ends and, according to the Bible, 'Vengeance is mine; I will repay, saith the Lord' (Romans 12:19), a Christian's duty is to suffer the slings and arrows of outrageous fortune and trust that God will in his own time bring the wrongdoer to justice. 'Patience is the honest man's revenge' is how a character in Cyril Tourneur's *The Atheist's Tragedy* puts it. Furthermore, private revenge, being outside the law, is necessarily a crime: the avenger becomes a criminal and must himself be brought to justice. Killing for revenge means you are a murderer and must yourself be killed: revenge is therefore a form of suicide. And suicide is another repeated motif in the play – Hamlet's first and third soliloquies are meditations upon suicide, Horatio tries, but fails, to commit suicide, and Ophelia, wittingly or unwittingly, succeeds. The Stoic philosophy, which is invoked approvingly in a number of plays in the 1590s, was believed to require of its followers a willingness to commit suicide rather than fall into the hands of their enemies and compromise their values. When Hamlet expresses his admiration of Horatio's unmoved response to good and bad fortune, and when Horatio expresses the wish to be more an antique Roman than a Dane, the values and code Horatio espouses are those of Stoicism. Christianity, on the other hand, treats suicide as the greatest sin. So the play, like other tragedies of the period, explores the alternative value-systems of the classical and Christian worlds as perceived by a late-Elizabethan playwright, partly because all revenge tragedies challenge the Christian ethos and partly because there is a fascinating closeness between the code of self-abnegation embodied in Christ's death on the cross and the code of self-abnegation embodied in the Stoic's suicide.

In the end, meanings will always reflect the tastes of those who find them. Some critics are on the look-out for the moral lessons they can learn from literature – and for them *Hamlet* is a source of endless debate. A story about someone who sets out to avenge his father's death, but, in the process of tracking down and killing the murderer, brings about the deaths of five other people including his mother and then loses his own life, does not necessarily raise questions about the morality and practicality of the revenge code, but it certainly could. And because it could, these critics try to make sure that it does.

What, if they are right, are the values upheld by Shakespeare's play? There is considerable temptation to read Hamlet himself as not only the focus of these values but their spokesman too. But the Hamlet who emerges from a reading or performance of the play varies according to the reader, the actor or the audience. It has often been felt that Hamlet is a refined intellectual with a sensitive sensibility. Indeed, part of what Shakespeare seems to have done to his source is locate a number of characters (not only Hamlet, but Horatio, Rosencrantz, Guildenstern, and Laertes too) as students – even Polonius harks back to his days at the university. Early on Hamlet refers to Horatio's 'philosophy'; late on he seems to be full of respect for something, at least, in his friend's philosophical position. We don't have to assume that Shakespeare had imagined a coherent framework of belief for this rather minor character. Rather, it seems to work the other way round, telling us of Hamlet's interest in ideas: he is, after all, someone who comes on stage reading, like Brutus in *Julius Caesar* or the young courtiers in *Love's Labour's Lost*. His sensitivity is evidenced by his highly wrought emotional state in respect of his late father, his mother, his uncle, and his girl-friend, and the apparent lack of consistent commitment to the carrying out of the revenge, once he has been commissioned by the Ghost towards the end of Act I. He alludes to the operations of conscience, and this would seem to suggest that he has one.

However, as we have already said, at least one of the allusions has the effect of indicating his lack of conscience – Horatio seems to think that Hamlet might be regretting bringing about the deaths of Rosencrantz and Guildenstern, but Hamlet denies it. Similarly, Hamlet shows no remorse over the death of Polonius – or, indeed, anyone much that he kills. The Hamlet who rails at Ophelia or Gertrude in private, and who embarrasses them in public, is cruel, even sadistic, and the Hamlet who taunts Polonius, Rosencrantz, Guildenstern, and Claudius is not a particularly nice piece of work either, however justified we may feel he is in treating them as his enemies.

All of the preceding remarks assume that the story which Shakespeare came up with is a fixed entity, Shakespeare's *Hamlet*. But this is far from the case. There are any number of entities which have or will have a claim to be that.

In 1602 the Stationers' Company (the official organization of Elizabethan printers and publishers) registered 'A booke called the Revenge of Hamlett Prince of Denmarke'. We cannot be sure whether or not this text was by Shakespeare, but the following year saw the publication of a play described on its title-page as *The Tragicall Historie of Hamlet Prince of Denmarke By William Shake-speare*. This, the earliest known text of an Elizabethan play about Hamlet, is printed in quarto (a format approximating to the dimensions of this book), and is known by Shakespearian scholars as the First Quarto (or Q1) of *Hamlet*.

Scholars were ignorant of Q1 until 1823, when a copy was discovered by Sir Henry Bunbury. At first it was taken to be a printing of Shakespeare's first draft of his play. But in 1843 the bibliographical scholar John Payne Collier published his view that, on the contrary, it was a poor attempt by unscrupulous actors or members of the audience to make money out of Shakespeare's *Hamlet* by selling a text which recorded the words spoken on stage in an early public performance.

If Collier was right that Q1 is a pirated text – and, despite his notoriety as a bibliographical forger, most subsequent scholars have accepted Collier's theory – then a performance text would obviously have already been established before the compilers of Q1 got to work on it. In 1604 another, much longer and very different, version of *The Tragicall Historie of Hamlet* was printed by James Roberts. Scholars have long known of this, the Second Quarto (Q2). Since Roberts was the man who had got 'The Revenge of Hamlett' registered in 1602, it seems possible that he was thereby trying vainly to prevent anyone pirating *Hamlet* before he could get his text of the play published. If this is correct, then Q2 may really be a record of a text which pre-dates Q1, or even the text upon which Q1 is based.

Q2 has striking differences from Q1, particularly after what we now call Act I: it is 'enlarged' to 3,674 lines and by a number of new scenes, the names of some characters are changed (Corambis becomes 'Polonius', Montano 'Reynaldo', Rossencraft 'Rosencrantz', Gilderstone 'Guildenstern' and Albertius 'Gonzago'), and many speeches are profoundly recast – for example, Hamlet's soliloquy beginning

> To be, or not to be, I there's the point,
> To Die, to sleepe, is that all? I all

which becomes

> To be, or not to be, that is the question:
> Whether 'tis nobler in the mind to suffer
> The slings and arrows of outrageous fortune,
> Or to take arms against a sea of troubles,
> And by opposing, end them. To die, to sleep –
> No more . . .

> (III. i. 57–62)

Q2 was reprinted with only minor alterations in 1611 (Q3) and 1622 (Q4).

Then, in 1623, the play appeared in yet another version – as

The Tragedie of Hamlet in the First Folio (a larger format than a quarto) edition of Shakespeare's works. This text (known as F1) is a bit shorter than Q2, omitting 222 lines but adding eighty-three new lines and a number of other smaller variations.

The lines omitted are concentrated in just six scenes but include some well-known passages: eighteen lines about the ominous significance of ghosts go in I. i and I. iv, including the lines about the 'vicious mole of nature' which Olivier used to introduce his 1948 film of the play; twenty-seven of Hamlet's lines to his mother in III.iv, including "'tis the sport to have the enginer | Hoist with his own petard'; all but the first eight lines of IV. iv, so that there is nothing of Hamlet quizzing the Norwegian captain about Fortinbras and then nothing of the soliloquy in which Hamlet compares himself unfavourably to that delicate and tender prince, 'How all occasions to inform against me'; twenty-five lines of Claudius plotting with Laertes in IV.vii, including his reflection that 'That we would do, | We should do when we would; for this "would" changes'; and fifty-four lines in the final scene, including most of what Osric and Hamlet have to say about Laertes. Most of the lines added are in II. ii, when Hamlet first remeets his old school-friends Rosencrantz and Guildenstern and informs them of his feeling that living in Denmark is like living in prison. While this idea has been gratefully siezed upon by twentieth-century directors, particularly in Eastern Europe, few actors have ever been allowed to use one of F1's additions – the 'O, o, o, o' with which he follows up his dying announcement, 'The rest is silence'.

It is galling for admirers of the most famous play in the world to have to admit that there are three *Hamlets*, and that editors have never succeeded in persuading one another which of the three is the 'real' Shakespearian text, the text to print and annotate and interpret. Editors have either tried to choose one of the three and print it as it stands or else they have selected passages from more than one and created their own *Hamlet*, a so-called 'eclectic' text. In fact, apart from those who have merely provided their readers with a photographic reproduction or diplomatic reprint of an existing copy of Q1, Q2 or F1, none has been prepared to resist meddling with and 'improving' the text. And when they emend the text in front of them, they are usually motivated by the desire to uncover a phantom text – the text which they claim is Shakespeare's and not an Elizabethan printer's, the text which lies behind Q1, Q2, and F1.

But what are they talking about when they refer to the text which lies behind one of these printed books? Do they have in mind a *manuscript*, perhaps, either in Shakespeare's hand or copied by a professional scribe employed by the theatre or by the printer? Or are they talking about a *performance* of the play? Few, until recently, have ever meant the latter. But the trouble with trying to recapture the performance text is that no two performances of a play are identical. So which performance are they trying to recapture? The first night (or afternoon, in *Hamlet*'s case)? Even if we could revisit it, perhaps things went wrong on the first performance and we would have been better served by a later performance in the run. The majority of editors have preferred to dream of a manuscript. But whichever text it is that they are after, there are problems associated with giving it any special importance. For the process by which a printed text of a play comes into being inevitably entails a sequence of 'texts' which precede it.

Think of the history of the manufacture of a manuscript. Following a very naïve theory of composition we could try to imagine a completed text of *Hamlet* which existed in Shakespeare's imagination before he wrote anything down. That might be the text with which we wish to compare Q1. But even if we believed that such a text existed at some moment before 19 May 1603, we can never have any access to it. It is a useless act of our imagination to try to conceive of it. And anyway, it is an improbable fiction. More credible is a scenario in which Shakespeare had certain ideas and developed them as he wrote. But the earliest such text of the play would be difficult to 'freeze', being something which evolved over days, weeks or even years. However long the process, it becomes impossible within such a scenario to talk about *one* text until it finally all gets written down. Even then, it would probably get altered by its author as he noticed errors or thought of ways of improving it. If there ever were such a manuscript and by some lucky chance it still existed and had been found, a modern scholar would be faced with more than one state of the text, each crossing out and emendation creating a new text of a play continuing to evolve. Which of these texts would an editor choose?

Usually editors try to choose the most 'authorial' text, and that usually means the earliest. But supposing the choice is as described – between texts all of which have a claim to be authorial? Earliest ceases to be the automatic choice. Indeed, an editor might wish to identify as the preferred text the latest version of it, with all Shakespeare's emendations replacing his earlier thoughts or errors. At first glance, this seems a sensible principle. But further examination reveals that there is no sound reason to adopt it. If an editor adopted such a principle it would have to be either an arbitrary act of commitment based on no deeper principle than the need to have a principle, or else a belief that authors always improve when they revise. And there is no evidence or logical reason to support that second principle. Was Wordsworth's revised version of *The Prelude* finer than his first version? Some readers think so. Others don't. Similarly, some readers or audiences may prefer the Folio text of *King Lear* to the Quarto version. That is their privilege. The Oxford *Complete Works* prints both, claiming that they are both authorial and leaving it to the reader rather than the editor to choose the better text.

3

Hamlet and History

The history of *Hamlet* as a text or series of texts is as we have seen in chapter 2 a complex narrative in itself. The post-history or afterlife of *Hamlet* as a literary or cultural phenomenon of enormous proportions is something we have raised in chapter 1 and will return to in chapter 6. Here, we shall address two other aspects of the play's relation to history and politics: *Hamlet* as a self-contained fiction which takes history and politics as part of its subject matter, and *Hamlet* as a late-Elizabethan play which can be seen in relation to the history and politics of its own time. This second topic is one which has been of particular interest to recent critics of the 'new historicist' school, and we shall be looking at some of their readings.

Hamlet himself sees the task imposed on him by the Ghost as more than a merely personal act of revenge, complaining

> The time is out of joint – O cursed spite,
> That ever I was born to set it right!

(I. v. 188–9)

Editors gloss 'the time' here as meaning 'things generally' or 'the state of society', with reference to circumstances in Elsinore two months after the death of Hamlet's father. Later, Hamlet makes a general claim about the relationship between the theatre and the real world:

> the purpose of playing . . . was and is . . . to show . . . the very age and body of the time his form and pressure. (III. ii. 20–4)

The theatre imitates life, or, as he also puts it in this speech, holds 'the mirror up to nature' (III. ii. 22). Again, the generality of the expression ('the very age and body of the time') indicates that the claim goes beyond the personal. What kind of 'time' is involved here, and what kind of society? The earlier narrative of Hamlet or rather Amleth was as we have seen a primitive pre-Christian legend of murder and revenge featuring some graphically savage details, but Shakespeare's version is set in a sophisticated and Christian Renaissance court. While Shakespeare emphasizes that this is a particular foreign country in such matters as the relationship between Denmark and Norway and the notion of an elected monarchy, he draws on the late-sixteenth-century stereotype of the Danes as heavy drinkers (I. iv. 10–22), and encourages his audience to believe that the England to which Hamlet is sent and where all the men are mad (V. i. 154–5) is not very remote from their own time-frame. But how far is Shakespeare's *Hamlet* a political tragedy, how far a personal one? Many nineteenth- and twentieth-century critics have tended to neglect the political dimension of the play in favour of the personal one, preferring to see Hamlet as a sort of intellectual Everyman, an ineffectual outsider in a corrupt society, rather than as a Renaissance prince, but these dimensions need not be mutually exclusive. A brief survey of Act I will outline some of the complexities of the interaction between the personal and the political spheres.

The play's opening scene conveys an atmosphere of political instability. The sentinels seem nervous, as if they expect to be attacked; they feel the need to identify themselves as 'Friends to this ground' and 'liegemen to the Dane' (I. i. 15). The Ghost appears in armour – specifically the armour worn by the late king in a famous battle against Norway – and Horatio at once assumes that 'This bodes some strange eruption to our state' (l. 69), going on to detail the threatened military action of young Fortinbras, against which urgent and unusual preparations are in hand, as the most likely 'fear'd event' to which the Ghost is 'prologue' (l. 121–3). He cites the appearance of ghosts in ancient Rome 'A little ere the mightiest Julius fell' (l. 114) as an analogy, and desires the Ghost on its reappearance

If thou art privy to thy country's fate,
Which happily foreknowing may avoid,
O speak!

(ll. 133–5)

An audience or reader is likely to anticipate that a political drama is about to unfold, and this impression will be confirmed by the opening speech of I. ii, the new King's formal address to the court, apparently the first public occasion since his wedding with his brother's widow.

Many critics have found in this balanced and careful piece of rhetoric evidence of Claudius's self-assurance and political competence, but Hamlet's opening speeches reject the language of impersonal ritual and insist on private feeling as the touchstone for behaviour. His first soliloquy reveals the depth of his pain about his mother's hasty marriage, but he is also aware that it is dangerous in the current climate to reveal this: 'But break my heart, for I must hold my tongue' (I. ii. 159). The arrival of Horatio, Marcellus, and Barnardo at this point with their news of the Ghost complicates the public/private issue further in so far as Horatio, who seemed in I. i to be a military man, resident in Elsinore and a regular member of the watch with an insider's knowledge of local politics, now appears as Hamlet's friend and fellow student on a short visit from Wittenberg. This inconsistency or shift in the role of Hamlet's chief confidant perhaps signals a change in emphasis from the political to the more personal significance of what he reveals. The speculation about the Ghost's appearance relating to a forthcoming conflict with Norway is not repeated, and Hamlet's comments at the end of the scene are unspecific: 'I doubt some foul play . . . Foul deeds will rise, | Though all the earth o'erwhelm them, to men's eyes' (ll. 255–7).

In the next scene – a domestic one with Laertes, Ophelia, and Polonius – a further source of potential conflict between public obligation and private feeling for Hamlet is revealed in the concern of her brother and her father that Ophelia should not take the prince's declarations of love too seriously. Laertes warns her that, even if Hamlet is sincere, 'His greatness weigh'd, his will is not his own' (I. iii. 17), and that he cannot make his own choice of a partner further 'Than the main voice of Denmark goes withal' (l. 28). Polonius assumes more brutally that Hamlet is simply trying to seduce her, that his vows are mere 'springes to catch wood-cocks' (l. 115) and should not be believed. All this advice is revealed to be misguided by Gertrude's sad remark at Ophelia's funeral – 'I hop'd thou shouldst have been my Hamlet's wife' (V. i. 244) – but it serves to complicate the situation considerably at this point, particularly in relation to the issue of Hamlet's madness and whether its origins are political or private.

Hamlet's encounter with the Ghost, which takes up the remainder of the first Act (I. iv and v), is seen as a threat to his sanity in a number of ways. Horatio counsels him not to follow it:

> What if it tempt you toward the flood, my lord,
> Or to the dreadful summit of the cliff
> That beetles o'er his base into the sea,
> And there assume some other horrible form
> Which might deprive your sovereignty of reason,
> And draw you into madness?

(I. iv. 69–74)

The Ghost himself hints at tales of 'the secrets of my prison- house' which would 'harrow up thy soul, freeze thy young blood, | Make thy two eyes like stars start from their spheres' (I. v. 14–17), but, after a highly emotional account of his murder, centred far more on the 'falling off' of Gertrude than on the political motivation or consequences, he urges Hamlet to 'Taint not thy mind' in taking revenge (l. 85), apparently warning him against some mental or moral corruption. Finally, Hamlet, without telling his companions what the Ghost has revealed to him, warns them that 'I perchance hereafter shall think meet | To put an antic disposition on' (ll. 171–2).

In earlier versions of the story, as we have seen, Hamlet's or Amleth's feigned madness is explicitly a politically motivated device to protect himself and avert suspicion from his revenge plot, but it is not so clear in Shakespeare. In the next scene (some time having passed) we get Ophelia's distressed account of Hamlet's behaviour in her closet (II. i. 74–97) which Polonius confidently interprets as 'the very ecstasy of love' (l. 99). His attempt to demonstrate this to the King, however, by setting up the occasion on which they spy on an encounter between Hamlet and Ophelia (III. i), is notably unconvincing: 'Love?' says the King 'His affections do not that way tend' (III. i. 162). Yet for playgoers and readers it can seem that while Hamlet feigns madness for political purposes, he is at most risk of seriously 'tainting his mind' in scenes with Ophelia and Gertrude.

It is not always easy to distinguish between the personal and the political in *Hamlet*. The King's first speech in I. ii represents Denmark as a person – 'our whole kingdom . . . contracted in one brow of woe' (ll. 3–4) – and simultaneously represents Gertrude as a political partner as much as a personal one: 'Th'imperial jointress to this warlike state' (l. 9). Laertes uses military metaphors in his advice to Ophelia – 'keep you in the rear of your affection, | Out of the shot and danger of desire' (I. iii. 34–5) – as does Polonius: 'Set your entreatments at a higher rate | Than a command to parle' (I. iii. 122–3). The Ghost describes the poison entering his body in terms of a building or town being invaded (I. v. 63–70). Throughout the play, we are constantly reminded that the royal family have bodies of more significance than those of ordinary people. As Rosencrantz puts it in his flattering speech to the King concerning the importance of the latter's safety in III. iii:

> The single and peculiar life is bound
> With all the strength and armor of the mind
> To keep itself from noyance, but much more
> That spirit upon whose weal depends and rests
> The lives of many. The cess of majesty
> Dies not alone, but like a gulf does draw
> What's near it with it. Or it is a massy wheel
> Fix'd on the summit of the highest mount,
> To whose huge spokes ten thousand lesser things
> Are mortis'd and adjoin'd, which when it falls,
> Each small annexment, petty consequence,
> Attends the boist'rous ruin. Never alone,
> Did the King sigh, but with a general groan.

(ll. 11–23)

In this context, Hamlet's obsession with Gertrude's sexuality takes on a political dimension since, as Leonard Tennenhouse puts it,

'To possess her body is to possess the state' ('Violence done to Women on the Renaissance Stage', in *The Violence of Representation*, 1989, p. 84). The notion of political power being inherent in the body of a woman might seem particularly appropriate in an Elizabethan tragedy, but Tennenhouse sees *Hamlet* and in particular 'The Murder of Gonzago' as an effort 'to represent the queen's body as an illegitimate source of political authority':

> Hamlet's attempt at staging a play is very much an attempt on the playwright's part to imagine a situation in which political power was not associated with a female and the aristocratic female was not iconically bonded to the land. (p. 91)

He argues that it is important for Hamlet to distinguish two separate acts of treason, the seizing of the queen's body and the seizing of political power, since it is only by separating them and by subordinating the former that the threat to the state can be diminished:

> Hamlet's obsession with the misuse of the queen's sexuality, more than with his uncle's possession of the state, transforms the threat of dismemberment into pollution. We might say that, in redefining the nature of the threat against the body politic, Hamlet attempts to stage a Jacobean tragedy. (p. 96)

Tennenhouse is a new historicist critic and it is striking how this recent mode of criticism which explicitly focuses on the political and social circumstances in which Shakespeare's texts were originally produced has had a great deal more to say about Jacobean texts than about Elizabethan ones. New historicist critics have been fascinated by the notion of absolute male power and have consequently found in James I, his court, and the cultural products associated with it, more fertile ground than in the earlier period; when they look at Elizabethan plays they look at Shakespeare's Histories where the monarchs are all men.

Just as Tennenhouse sees in *Hamlet* an attempt to stage a Jacobean tragedy, so one of the most recent versions of a reading of the play as 'topical' in a contemporary sense is Stuart M.

Kurland's 'Hamlet and the Scottish Succession' (in Studies in English Literature, 34, 1994) which argues not for specific historical parallels but for the more general relevance of the play to the late-Elizabethan anxiety over the succession, which was accompanied by fear of foreign intervention. Hamlet is a threat to the King not only as a private avenger but as a possible alternative ruler. While Kurland is confident that 'Unlike some modern readers, Shakespeare's audience would have been unlikely to see in Hamlet's story merely a private tragedy or in Fortinbras' succession to the Danish throne a welcome and unproblematic restoration of order' (p. 291), he reads the play as looking forward with some trepidation to the not yet certain accession of James I.

Two studies which do attempt to take more account of the Elizabethan historical and political context of Hamlet are those by Karin S. Coddon (in Renaissance Drama, XX, 1989) and Patricia Parker (in McDonald, ed., Shakespeare Reread, 1994). Karin Coddon is interested in relating the play to the decline and fall of Elizabeth's former favourite, Robert Devereux, Earl of Essex, who was finally executed in February 1601, though his star had been declining since 1597 and he had notably lost the Queen's favour over his disastrous military expedition to Ireland in 1599 (prematurely and perhaps unwisely celebrated by Shakespeare in the Chorus to Act V of Henry V). Coddon explores the question of Essex's melancholy or madness, seen at the time as a product of thwarted ambition which became displaced into treason. Hamlet after all complains 'I lack advancement' (III. ii. 340), a remark which is closely followed by the King's pious justification of dispatching him to England on the grounds that in Denmark he is a threat to the security of the state (III. iii. 1–26). Without wanting to make an exact equation between the fictional Hamlet and the historical Essex, Coddon sees the representation of madness in the play as relating to the 'faltering of ideological prescriptions to define, order, and constrain subjectivity' (p. 61) and she argues for madness as 'an instrument of social and political disorder' (p. 62).

Patricia Parker's sense of the topical relevance of the play is quite different. Beginning with Hamlet's obsession with the 'secret places' of women – not only his interest in Gertrude's sexuality but his obscene references to Ophelia's 'lap' in the dialogue before the dumb show in III. ii – she moves into a reading which brings out the play's representation of a court full of spies and informers. The King employs Rosencrantz and Guildenstern to spy on Hamlet, to 'pluck out the heart of [his] mystery' (III. ii. 365–6), Polonius sends Reynaldo to spy on Laertes in Paris (II. i), and there are many instances of secrets being hidden or revealed. Parker sees *Hamlet* as being written at a 'crucial historical juncture' (p. 131) when a state secret service was being developed:

> This sense of both the holding and the withholding of secrets in *Hamlet* . . . [evokes] the emergent world of statecraft contemporary with the play, one that historians describe as increasingly involving the mediation of agents, go-betweens, and representatives across bureaucratic as well as geographic distances, along with the corresponding multiplication of informers and spies. (pp. 134–5)

If a political interpretation of this kind was topical around 1600, it has also seemed relevant when *Hamlet* has been staged more recently in countries where there has been a real fear of the secret police, such as the former Soviet Union and Eastern Europe, as we shall see in chapter 6. In the West, *Hamlet* has on the contrary been 'privatized', as R. A. Foakes has shown, beginning with the Romantics who abstracted the central character from the play and made possible the development of 'Hamletism', a sort of philosophical stance embodying political impotence, frustration, futility, and failure (Foakes, *'Hamlet' versus 'Lear'*, 1993, pp. 12–44). It still seems difficult for us to get away from this overwhelming focus on subjectivity and a vague modern kind of 'alienation' and to restore a sense of Hamlet in relation to a specific social or political context.

New historicist criticism has not really helped us in this endeavour, perhaps partly because of its own notorious insistence on the impossibility of meaningful political resistance or subversion. In her essay '"The Very Age and Body of the Time His Form and Pressure": Rehistoricizing Shakespeare's Theater', Annabel Patterson conducts something of a critique of new historicist readings of Shakespeare's political plays and indeed Shakespeare's politics. She questions the simplistic polarizations suggested by recent work on the likely composition of his audiences – were they 'popular' or 'privileged'? – and challenges the pessimistic view of the playwright and his theatre as merely serving the Elizabethan and Jacobean state apparatus. While allowing that it would be naïve to assume that Shakespeare's theories concerning the nature and function of drama are the same as those expressed by Hamlet in his discussion with the Players, she nevertheless re-examines those speeches for what they can tell us about the relationship between the theatre and its historical and political context. Hamlet after all virtually threatens Polonius with the power of the actors to comment on public figures:

> Let them be well us'd, for they are the abstract and brief chronicles of the time. After your death you were better have a bad epitaph than their ill report while you live. (II. ii. 523–6)

Such a speech would hardly make sense in a theatre which had succeeded in banning topical allusions or in one which was seen as politically impotent or subservient to the state. Hamlet is making a strong claim here for the significance or effectiveness of the actors' 'report' – what they say about people – though, as we shall see in the next chapter, he himself has an ambivalent relationship to the power of language.

4

Words, Words, Words

It is difficult, given our acquaintance with a post-Elizabethan, 'universal' *Hamlet*, to imagine what it would have been like to encounter Shakespeare's version of the Hamlet story as a new play in the social and political context of 1600. Moreover, not just the story but many of the words and phrases of *Hamlet* are already familiar, indeed over-familiar, to the modern playgoer or reader. It can seem a tissue of quotations, including, for example, the following:

A little more than kin, and less than kind!	(I. ii. 65)
One may smile, and smile, and be a villain	(I. v. 108)
There are more things in heaven and earth, Horatio, Than are dreamt of in your philosophy.	(I. v. 166–7)
The time is out of joint – O cursed spite, That ever I was born to set it right!	(I. v. 188–9)
What a piece of work is a man	(II. ii. 303–4)
'Twas caviare to the general.	(II. ii. 436–7)
To be, or not to be, that is the question	(III. i. 57)
The undiscover'd country, from whose bourn No traveller returns	(III. i. 78–9)
The purpose of playing . . . is to hold . . . the mirror up to nature	(III. ii. 20–2)
'Tis the sport to have the enginer Hoist with his own petard	(III. iv. 206–7)
There's a divinity that shapes our ends	(V. ii. 10)

All these lines and many more have passed into common usage, leaving performers of the play with the problem of how to make them sound fresh, as if spoken for the first time, and how to make them sound as if they arise naturally from their context, not like quotations from some previous work. Hamlet's soliloquies in particular challenge the actor in this way, especially if he is aware of members of the audience alerting each other to a 'purple passage', or even speaking it with him. John Gielgud tried in his 1934 performance to deliver 'To be or not to be' as a kind of inner monologue, but found it difficult to ignore the audience because 'frequently one can hear words and phrases being whispered by people in the front rows, just before one is going to speak them' (quoted in Mary Z. Maher, *Modern Hamlets and their Soliloquies*, 1992, p. 9). In a recent television interview Kevin Kline spoke of this as the 'singalongaHamlet' phenomenon (*Playing the Dane*, broadcast on BBC2, 9 October 1994). It is almost impossible for today's students to believe that the compilers of the 1603 First Quarto of *Hamlet* (if that does indeed represent someone's memory of a performance) apparently managed to forget the second half of this most famous line, recording it as 'To be, or not to be, I [Ay] there's the point'.

The fact that *Hamlet* is so much quoted is obviously related to its longlasting canonical status, but not only that. It seems significant that all the above lines are spoken by Hamlet himself: he is represented as a reflective character, given to musing, philosophizing, generalizing from his own situation to larger issues. (However much *King Lear* may have taken over *Hamlet's* place in the hierarchy of Shakespeare's tragedies, its hero has fewer quotable lines.) Hamlet fills up the time between the revelations of the Ghost and the killing of Claudius, not with plotting ingenious and appropriate methods of punishment for his enemy like other revengers, but with a great deal of talking; famous for his monologues, he is also one of the theatre's most engaged and engaging conversationalists. He discourses at length about his own melancholy to Rosencrantz and Guildenstern in II. ii, he lectures Ophelia on the use of cosmetics in III. i, he discusses the art of acting with the Players in III. ii, he reflects on mortality in IV. iii (despite the King's minimal, unencouraging responses) and returns to this theme in V.i. Claudius finds his verbosity infuriating (in IV. iii he just wants to know what has happened to the body of Polonius), and this response can be shared by an audience, as for example when Hamlet is more interested in exchanging witticisms with the Gravedigger in V. i than in focusing on the fact (painfully obvious to us) that this is the grave of Ophelia. At other times it can seem touching, as in the good-humoured mocking of Osric in V.ii, sandwiched between grimly stoical reflections on his own forthcoming death. (Shakespeare himself may have felt, however, that this last passage was excessive and self-indulgent, either on his own part or on that of Hamlet, since some thirty-five lines of it are cut in the Folio text.)

'Suit the action to the word, the word to the action' (III. ii. 17–18). One of Hamlet's problems of course is that he is better at words than at actions. Or at least that he does not get on with the important action – the killing of the King. It may seem to us as spectators or readers that he is busy enough with other things, but, moved by the First Player's rendition of 'Aeneas' tale to Dido' (II. ii. 446) with its description of the killing of Priam and the extravagant grief of Hecuba, he deplores first his own relative inactivity and then his tendency to 'like a whore unpack my heart with words' (II. ii. 585). (As we shall see in chapter 5, Hamlet associates verbosity with femininity.) He is acutely sensitive to language: on his first appearance in I. ii he has two one-line puns or verbal quibbles – 'A little more than kin, and less than kind' and 'Not so, my lord, I am too much in the sun' – followed by an eleven-line discourse on outward show versus inner reality which picks up on Gertrude's use of the word 'seems' (I. ii. 65, 67, 76–86). His contempt for mere hollow behaviour – 'actions that a man might play' – is however later contradicted by his advice to his mother to 'Assume a virtue if you have it not', where he argues that pretending to wish to abstain from sex with the King will make actual abstinence easier to achieve (III. iv. 160–7).

Other characters are also sensitive to issues relating to the relations between thoughts, words, and deeds. The King comments ruefully on his own insincere attempt to repent:

> My words fly up, my thoughts remain below:
> Words without thoughts never to heaven go.

> (III. iii. 97–8)

The Gravedigger insists on precise literal meanings: 'How absolute the knave is!' comments Hamlet, 'we must speak by the card, or equivocation will undo us' (V. i. 137–8). The King insists that Gertrude provides words to supplement her gestures of distress after her closet interview with Hamlet –

> There's matter in these sighs. These profound heaves –
> You must translate, 'tis fit we understand them.

> (IV. i. 1–2)

An anonymous Gentleman describes the difficulty of interpreting the language Ophelia speaks in her madness, when her words seem disconnected from her thoughts:

>   Her speech is nothing.
> Yet the unshaped use of it doth move
> The hearers to collection; they yawn at it,
> And botch the words up fit to their own thoughts,
> Which as her winks and nods and gestures yield them,
> Indeed would make one think there might be thought,
> Though nothing sure, yet much unhappily.

> (IV. v. 7–13)

Laertes however remarks later in the scene 'This nothing's more than matter' (IV. v. 174).

The play as a whole insists on the vital importance of speech to enlighten and elucidate the world from the first scene where Horatio is asked to make sense of the Ghost by talking to it – 'Thou art a scholar, speak to it, Horatio' (I. i. 42) – to the last where the same character becomes Hamlet's 'mouth' (V. ii. 392) for the newly arrived Norwegians and English, fulfilling the dying prince's request that he should live a little longer in order to 'tell my story' (V. ii. 349). It is particularly appropriate that Hamlet's own last words (and in stage tradition often the last words of the play) are 'the rest is silence' (V. ii. 358).

Moreover, not just any speech or words will serve. 'That's an ill phrase, a vile phrase, "beautified" is a vile phrase' says Polonius (II. ii. 111–12), breaking off from reading Hamlet's letter to Ophelia to comment on its literary style, much to the frustration of the King and Gertrude who have been urging him to get to the point he has promised to make about Hamlet's madness, to give them 'More matter, with less art' (II. ii. 95). Usually played as tedious and long-winded himself, Polonius nevertheless objects to the First Player's speech – 'This is too long' (II. ii. 498). *Hamlet* is a play which has time to draw attention to its own linguistic structures in a way which perhaps relates it to Shakespeare's earlier, more rhetorical tragedies, *Titus Andronicus* and *Romeo and Juliet*, rather than to the later ones such as *Othello* and *Macbeth*. The numerous differences and complex relationships between the surviving texts of *Hamlet* seem to indicate (at least) that the author rewrote many passages, cutting, inserting, rearranging, and revising.

In Shakespeare's time, literary genres such as tragedy and comedy were, in theory, governed by a Renaissance version of classical rhetoric whereby certain vocabularies and styles of expression were thought to be suitable to certain modes of writing: a 'high' style was appropriate to tragedy, a 'low' style to comedy. Modern critics such as Marion Trousdale (*Shakespeare and the Rhetoricians*, 1982) and Jane Donawerth (*Shakespeare and the Sixteenth-Century Study of Language*, 1984) have demonstrated the extent to which Shakespeare's works were shaped by contemporary views about language and contemporary methods of rhetorical training. Despite Shakespeare's willingness to break neo-classical rules in other matters (such as his famous disregard of the 'unities' of place and time), his plays do show some evidence of this kind of literary decorum: in *Hamlet*, for example, lower-class characters such as the Gravedigger and his companion (designated 'Clowns' in all three early printed texts) speak in prose – but Hamlet also speaks in prose with his courtier/student friends Rosencrantz and Guildenstern and with the super-courtly Osric.

It should however be emphasized that this does not mean that each character has his or her own distinctive mode of speech. What sometimes seems difficult for modern audiences and readers to grasp is that with this and other Shakespearian tragedies the heightening of the style is related to the style of the play as a whole, not to the specific speech of any given character. Hamlet may have more 'memorable lines' than other characters but that is to a large extent an index of the fact that he has a larger part. When it comes to metaphorical language, puns, and other forms of verbal heightening or wordplay, he simply draws, albeit more frequently and perhaps at times more deeply, on a resource which is generally available to all the characters. When critics write studies of the 'imagery' of *Hamlet*, perhaps exploring the many references to disease or to the human body, they have to acknowledge that any character, from the King to an anonymous Gentleman or Clown, can adumbrate the play's concerns impersonally, as it were, or chorically. To take a particularly striking example, we should not imagine that when the King refers apprehensively to Laertes as one who

> wants not buzzers to infect his ear
> With pestilent speeches of his father's death

> (IV. v. 90–1)

he is consciously alluding to his own crime of murdering Old Hamlet by pouring poison into his ear; we accept that he is merely contributing to the play's overall pattern of literal and metaphorical references to ears and acts of aggression performed against them. For Shakespeare and for the audience these do indeed arise from the literal circumstance of the murder, but most of the characters who speak such lines are not aware of their significance.

All the characters then speak the same language as Hamlet in so far as they all speak the language of *Hamlet*. This is a language densely packed with meaning, unusually rich in puns, quibbles, and other forms of wordplay, as M. M. Mahood has shown (Mahood, *Shakespeare's Wordplay*, 1957). Line after line could evoke Benedick's triumphant discovery that 'there's a double meaning in that!' (*Much Ado About Nothing*, II. iii. 258). Polonius quibbles self-consciously in his first conversation with Ophelia when she has told him about the 'tenders of affection' made to her by Hamlet:

> Think yourself a baby
> That you have ta'en these tenders for true pay
> Which are not sterling. Tender yourself more dearly,
> Or – not to crack the wind of the poor phrase,
> Running it thus – you'll tender me a fool.

> (I. iii. 105–9)

Part of Hamlet's procedure in putting on his 'antic disposition' is to quibble in this way, pretending not to understand Polonius:

POLONIUS What do you read, my lord?
HAMLET Words, words, words.
POLONIUS What is the matter, my lord?
HAMLET Between who?
POLONIUS I mean the matter that you read, my lord . . .
POLONIUS (*aside*) Though this be madness, yet there is method in't. – Will you walk out of the air, my lord?
HAMLET Into my grave?
POLONIUS Indeed, that's out of the air.

(II. ii. 191–208)

He employs a similar verbal strategy against Ophelia when they are watching 'The Mousetrap':

HAMLET Lady, shall I lie in your lap?
OPHELIA No, my lord.
HAMLET I mean, my head upon your lap?
OPHELIA Ay, my lord.
HAMLET Do you think I meant country matters?
OPHELIA I think nothing, my lord.
HAMLET That's a fair thought – to lie between maids' legs.

(III. ii. 112–9)

In this instance Hamlet is teasing (or, more sadistically, taunting) Ophelia with the possibilities for obscene double meanings in his language – possibilities which Shakespeare is always alert to in a way that can astonish the modern reader.

Quibbles can be straightforwardly comic, edgily comic, or even deadly serious, as when Hamlet encounters his father's ghost for the first time:

Thou com'st in such a questionable shape
That I will speak to thee.

(I. iv. 43–4)

Or when he finally forces the King to drink the poison, saying 'Is thy union here? | Follow my mother' (V. ii. 326–7), punning grimly on 'union' meaning both the large pearl the King has put into the cup (presumably disguising or containing the poison, or just identifying the cup as Hamlet's; V. ii. 272–83) and his marriage to Gertrude.

Modern attempts to pay proper attention to the linguistic detail of Shakespeare's plays have to contend with at least three separate areas of difficulty. Firstly, we have lost the rhetorical training of Shakespeare's time and the rhetorical vocabulary that went with it: very few people today know what an anaphora is, or a chiasmus, or a paranomasia, and most people suspect that the labelling of figures of speech in this way is a dead (and deadening) art. Secondly, we are aware that the language of drama as it is performed is more than just the language of the literary text or script; other, non-verbal meanings can be just as important and must be taken into account. Thirdly, we are unwilling to examine details of language for their own sake; we immediately want to ask how they affect 'the meaning of the play', leaping from the particular intricacy of a line or passage to a character- or theme-based generalization.

There are, despite these problems, some valuable studies of the language of *Hamlet*. In addition to the books on Renaissance rhetoric mentioned above, some critics have successfully demonstrated the links between the verbal design of the play and its thematic patterns and stage-pictures: Maurice Charney, for example, in *Style in 'Hamlet'* (1969) and Nigel Alexander in *Poison, Play and Duel* (1971). A more ambitious and technical approach is attempted by Keir Elam in his section on *Hamlet* in *The Semiotics of Theatre and Drama* (1980) in which he offers a 'dramatological score' of the first seventy-nine lines of the play, using a notation system borrowed from linguistics. Several of the contributors to *Shakespeare Reread* (edited by Russ McDonald, 1994) refer to *Hamlet* in their discussions of the place of 'traditional close reading' in relation to modern 'literary theory'.

George T. Wright's essay on 'Hendiadys and *Hamlet*' (in *Publications of the Modern Language Association*, 96, 1981) is both a rare attempt to revivify and promote an almost forgotten rhetorical figure and an interesting example of the attempt to move from the microlevel of language to the macrolevel of thematic analysis. We feel it deserves serious attention on both counts. Wright begins by arguing that it is important for us to be aware of hendiadys because Shakespeare uses it over 300 times in all, 'mainly in the great plays of his middle career and most of all in *Hamlet*'. Hendiadys means literally 'one through two'. Wright defines it conventionally as 'the use of two substantives, joined by a conjunction, to express a single but complex idea' (p. 168), citing as a classic example the line in Vergil's *Georgics* (II. 192): *pateris libamus et auro* – 'we drink from cups and from gold' – simplifiable (albeit reductively) in translation to 'we drink from golden cups'. It is necessary that the two entities being joined should be related but not in exact parallel: there is something odd, unexpected, even uneasy about hendiadys, as if the relationship between the terms does not quite fit. But this can make the resulting expression more intense, as in Edmund's 'nothing like the image and horror of it' (*King Lear*, I. ii. 175), as compared with 'nothing like the horrible image of it', or Macbeth's 'full of sound and fury' (*Macbeth*, V. v. 27), as compared with 'full of furious sound'.

Wright finds sixty-six instances of hendiadys in *Hamlet*, far more than in any other play; *Othello* comes second with a mere twenty-five and only six other plays have more than ten examples (*Troilus and Cressida* has nineteen, *Macbeth* eighteen, *Measure for Measure* sixteen, *Henry V* and *King Lear* fifteen each, and *Twelfth Night* thirteen.) In *Hamlet* it occurs in both verse and prose, in almost every scene, and in the speech of every major character. Some striking examples are:

In the dead waste and middle of the night	(I. ii. 198)
Unto the voice and yielding of that body	(I. iii. 23)
Out of the shot and danger of desire	(I. iii. 35)
Th'expectation and rose of the fair state	(III. i. 152)
The very age and body of the time	(III. ii. 23–4)
So far from cheer and from your former state	(III. ii. 164)
No, in despite of sense and secrecy	(III. iv. 192)
That capability and godlike reason	(IV. iv. 38)

Which is not tomb enough and continent (IV. iv. 64)

Divided from herself and her fair judgment (IV. v. 86)

These and Wright's other examples are very interesting in themselves, and he does discuss several of them in satisfying detail, but he also attempts to relate hendiadys to the meaning of the play as a whole, as a 'miniature stylistic play within the play' (p. 181). He finds it being used by specific characters at specific moments: in Laertes' advice to Ophelia in I. iii, for example, 'his frequent hendiadys reveals his own uncertain and divided sensibility', while Polonius's use of the same figure in his instructions to Reynaldo about spying on his son seems to indicate his deviousness (p. 176). Wright goes on to develop a thematic analysis of the play's obsession with doublings and disjunctions, misleading dualisms and false parallels, claiming that such deceptive linkings are 'exactly what hendiadys expresses' (p. 178). While this is true, he also admits very honestly that 'readings based on hendiadys are sometimes not much at variance with traditional ones' (p. 182) – we always knew that *Hamlet* was concerned with these issues – as Horatio puts it 'There needs no ghost, my lord, come from the grave | To tell us this' (I. v. 125–6). The real value of this excellent essay is in the discovery of the play's detail, the analysis of its rhetorical complexity, not in the obligatory search for larger patterns of meaning.

5

Hamlet and Gender

'A female Hamlet is one thing but a pregnant prince is quite another' says Dora Chance in Angela Carter's novel *Wise Children* (1991). Dora and her identical twin sister Nora are stars of vaudeville and illegitimate daughters of Sir Melchior Hazard, the great Shakespearean actor. The novel contains many references to *Hamlet*, including the moment when the hero's most celebrated soliloquy becomes the inspiration for a song and dance routine with the two sisters dressed as bellhops in a hotel corridor, debating whether a package should be delivered to '2b or not 2b' (p. 90). The pregnant prince (in this case Dora's and Nora's grandmother Estella Hazard, pregnant with their natural father Melchior and his twin brother Peregrine, who passes for their father) belongs to the level of subversive fantasy and the cheerful appropriation of Shakespeare's texts by twentieth-century low culture, but in fact the notion of Hamlet as female has a lengthy history in the critical and theatrical reception of the play.

Hamlet himself, as we mentioned in chapter 4, sees his inaction in general and his verbosity in particular as effeminate in his soliloquy after his first encounter with the Players:

> Why, what an ass am I! This is most brave,
> That I, the son of a dear father murthered,
> Prompted to my revenge by heaven and hell,
> Must like a whore unpack my heart with words,
> And fall a-cursing like a very drab.

> (II. ii. 582–6)

As Patricia Parker points out in *Literary Fat Ladies*,

> In the traditional opposition of genders in which 'Women are words, men deeds', Hamlet's comparison of his verbal and deedless delay to

the impotent anger of a 'drab' [prostitute] sets up a link between his entire period of inactivity and delay and womanish wordiness, in contrast to such one-dimensional emblems of masculinity as Laertes and the aptly named Fort-in-bras [strong-in-arms]. (1987, p. 23)

Much later, just before the fatal duel with Laertes, Hamlet dismisses his sense of 'how ill all's here about my heart' as 'such a kind of gaingiving [misgiving], as would perhaps trouble a woman' (V. ii. 212–16). He sees his own behaviour and his capacity for feeling as more appropriate to a woman than to a man, but is behaving and feeling like a woman the same as being a woman? Fears about Hamlet's apparent lack of essential masculinity have often been expressed by critics who focus on his weakness, his vacillation, his melancholy – all seen as feminine traits. Goethe was apparently the first to say that Hamlet was 'part woman', and an extensive critical tradition draws on what now looks like fairly crude gender stereotyping to perpetuate this point. It came to a climax in 1881 with the publication of Edward P. Vining's book *The Mystery of Hamlet*, which developed the theory that in revising his play Shakespeare dallied with the idea that Hamlet was in fact born female and was educated from infancy to impersonate a male. This book inspired the fine silent film version directed in Germany by Sven Gade and Heinz Schall in 1920 in which Asta Nielsen played the hero precisely as a princess passed off as a prince by her mother, anxious to secure the succession when it is feared just as she is giving birth that Old Hamlet has been killed by Old Fortinbras (see Plate 5).

Those who have written about this film, both when it was released and more recently, have insisted on its distance from Shakespeare, though it is in fact closer to the text than they allow, and provides some fascinating reflections on gender issues in the play. But on the stage too a large number of women have acted Hamlet (as a man, that is), from Sarah Siddons in 1776 and Elizabeth Edmead in 1792 to at least Frances de la Tour in 1979 and Diane Venora in 1983. And these were not necessarily seen as freakish or one-off performances: Siddons played Hamlet in Birmingham, Manchester, Liverpool, Bristol, and Dublin between 1776 and 1802, while Millicent Bandmann-Palmer performed the part over a thousand times from 1887 to 1902; she is referred to in James Joyce's *Ulysses* when John Eglinton tells Stephen Daedalus that 'an actress played Hamlet for the fourhundredandeighth time last night in Dublin'. There was serious acclaim for actresses such as Charlotte Cushman (from 1848), Alice Marriott (from 1861) and Sarah Bernhardt (from 1899) in the role during the nineteenth century (see Jill Edmonds, 'Princess Hamlet', in Gardner and Rutherford, eds., *The New Woman and Her Sisters*, 1992).

Many of these women were in the position of actor-managers and could choose to play Hamlet simply because it was the best part available, but they also exploited what was seen as a feminine ability to convey the interiority of the character and to do justice to Hamlet's romantic sensitivity. The dominant view of Hamlet as a poetic dreamer, played even by male actors as an aesthetic, even pre-Raphaelite figure, no doubt helped to make these interpretations acceptable. Eugène Delacroix apparently used a female model for his lithographs of Hamlet in 1834–45. (see Cover/Frontispiece and see Foakes, *'Hamlet' versus 'Lear'*, 1993, p. 23). By 1979 however Frances de la Tour's performance was admired for quite different qualities. As one reviewer put it: 'She is tough, abrasive, virile and impassioned. Indeed it's a good performance compact with every female virtue except femininity' (Michael Billington, *The Guardian*, 20 October 1979). Asked about the phenomenon of women playing Hamlet fifteen years later, de la Tour herself explained

> I think it is because it is universal youth, expressing all the emotions of youth and of life, and there isn't another part to match it . . . There would be no need and no desire for a woman to play Lear. It's not the same as Hamlet. (*The Observer Review Extra*, 9 October 1994, and BBC2 programme *Playing the Dane*, broadcast 30 October 1994)

But Hamlet's own misogyny remains an issue. 'Frailty, thy name is woman!' he says (I. ii. 146) when he is left alone on stage at the end of the second scene of the play to reflect on the speed with which his widowed mother has married his uncle. Later he exclaims 'O most pernicious woman!' (I. v. 105) on hearing the Ghost's tale of Gertrude's 'falling off' from the 'celestial bed' of her first marriage to the 'garbage' and 'damned incest' of her second (I. v. 56–7, 83). Similarly, he feels betrayed by Ophelia who in obedience to her father rejects his attentions and returns his letters and gifts. Reserving his idealization for men (his dead father and Horatio), he attacks both women vehemently, Ophelia in the 'nunnery' scene (III. i) and Gertrude in the 'closet' scene (III. iv), on both occasions evoking a somewhat baffled response in so far as the women do not seem to be absolutely clear what they are being accused of. Some editors and directors have felt it necessary to bring Hamlet onstage early in III. i so that he overhears Polonius and the King plotting to spy on him and his anger against Ophelia becomes motivated by her complicity in this. Ophelia herself clearly cannot understand his attitude but can only attribute it to madness (III. i. 151–62).

Gertrude, three scenes later, admits and regrets what she has already described as her 'o'erhasty marriage' (II. ii. 57), but seems sincerely shocked – 'As kill a king!' (III. iv. 30) – by her son's suggestion that she was actually implicated in the murder of her first husband. Curiously, they neither of them pursue this more serious charge which is also implied by the Player Queen's line 'None wed the second but who killed the first' (III. ii. 180), while the Ghost's repeated admonitions to Hamlet to 'Leave her to heaven' (I. v. 86) and to 'step between her and her fighting soul' (III. iv. 113) would seem if anything to attest to Gertrude's relative innocence. The focus is instead on Hamlet's disgust at his mother's sexual activity 'In the rank sweat of an enseamed bed' (III. iv. 92) and his insistence that she begin to practise celibacy: 'Let not the bloat king tempt you again to bed' (III. iv. 182).

Hamlet's priggish attitude here – 'You cannot call it love, for at your age | The heyday in the blood is tame, it's humble, | And waits upon the judgment' (III. iv. 68–70) has been endorsed by critics and editors who worry about Gertrude's age, and indeed Hamlet's since, as they see it, if he is really thirty as the Gravedigger says (V. i. 142–62), she must be too old to excite the King's interest. It seems typical of her opacity as a character, or perhaps of the play's refusal to present her other than through Hamlet's eyes, that we do not know what impact this conversation has on her. While she seems to accept Hamlet's harsh judgement in this scene, and to be prepared to obey his commands and keep his secrets, her relationship with the King through the remainder of the play seems unchanged – or at least there is no clear

45

indication in the text that they have become estranged, though some productions do play it in this way. Nor is it clear why in the last scene she becomes what Janet Adelman calls

> a wonderfully homey presence for her son, newly available to him as the loving and protective mother of his childhood, worrying about his condition, wiping his face as he fights, even perhaps intentionally drinking the poison intended for him. (*Suffocating Mothers*, 1992, p. 34)

The fact that this last suggestion has been made quite often, again without any clear warrant from the text, seems an indication of how baffled critics are by Gertrude. It is also an option in the stage tradition, though it is quite a challenge for the performer to convey this intention to the audience by meaningful looks at a point when attention is more likely to be focused on Hamlet. Nineteenth-century Gertrudes sometimes said 'I have [drunk]' rather than 'I will', apparently to soften the act of deliberate disobedience to the King, and even then might be sent offstage to die. The entire role was severely and quite consistently cut from 1755 to 1900 (and frequently after that) in such a way as to eliminate any possibility of Gertrude being affected by the closet scene encounter with Hamlet (see O'Brien, 'Revision by Excision', in *Shakespeare Survey 45*, 1992). The 1920 film goes to the other extreme from the self-sacrificing mother in having Gertrude deliberately prepare the poison for her daughter Hamlet who has by this time already been responsible for the death of the King.

The extent and nature of the guilt projected on to Gertrude and by association on to Ophelia and indeed all women has much exercised the play's psychoanalytic critics. Freud saw Hamlet as a hysteric and many Freudians have offered interpretations which tease out parricidal or matricidal motives. Ernest Jones provided the classic Oedipal reading of the play in 1949, arguing that Hamlet is unable to kill the King because he represents the fulfilment of Hamlet's own repressed erotic desire for his mother. In her essay on 'Sexuality in the Reading of Shakespeare' (in Drakakis, ed., *Alternative Shakespeares*) Jacqueline Rose traces how influential male readers of the play – T. S. Eliot as well as Ernest Jones and the Freudians – have echoed Hamlet's misogyny and blamed Gertrude for what they saw as the aesthetic and moral failings of the play overall. Picking up on Eliot's analogy for *Hamlet* as 'the Mona Lisa of literature', she argues that in his reading

> the question of the woman and the question of meaning go together. The problem with *Hamlet* is not just that the emotion it triggers is unmanageable and cannot be contained by the woman who is its cause, but that this excess of affect produces a problem of interpretation: how to read, or control by reading, a play whose inscrutability (like that of the *Mona Lisa*) has baffled – and seduced – so many critics. (pp. 97–8)

Femininity itself becomes the problem within the play, and within attempts to interpret it, but paradoxically femininity is also seen as the source of creativity and the very principle of the aesthetic process in other psychoanalytic readings in which the focus shifts from character to author: Shakespeare, unlike his hero, can be claimed to have effected a productive reconciliation with the feminine in his own nature.

Modern male editors of the play are not necessarily more enlightened when it comes to talking about the women. Harold Jenkins remarks condescendingly of Ophelia that, rejected by Hamlet, she has 'little left to do . . . but to bewail her virginity . . . Her tragedy of course is that Hamlet has left her treasure with her' (Arden 2, pp. 151–2). G. R. Hibbard quotes this approvingly, adding that, as a virgin, she dies 'unfulfilled'. Moreover, he says, 'It is Ophelia's tragic fate to pay the price in pain and suffering for Gertrude's sins' (this despite the fact that he is very confident she was not privy to the murder), and goes on, 'Woman's sexuality has evidently become an obsession with [Hamlet]; and to this extent at least he is genuinely mad' (Oxford edition, p. 51). Surely such a definition of madness would include a sizeable proportion of the men in any given audience of the play?

The fate of Ophelia, specifically the scene of her drowning ('There is a willow grows askaunt the brook') is paradoxically one of the most vivid, iconic moments in the play (see Plate 3). Paradoxically, because it is not of course staged but rather described by Gertrude in elaborate detail (IV. vii. 166–83), shocking perhaps to the naturalistically trained 'modern reader [who] cannot suppress his astonishment that Gertrude should have watched Ophelia die without lifting a finger to help her' (Edwards, New Cambridge edition, 1985, p. 212). It has become familiar through decorative, dreamy paintings such as the one by John Everett Millais in the Tate Gallery in London, and it does tend to be represented in film and video versions of the play; Eleuterio Rodolfi was clearly inspired by Millais for the depiction of the death of Ophelia in his 1917 film (which has Pre-Raphaelite decor throughout), as was Olivier in 1948. Unfortunately, suicide by drowning has also become a typically feminine death, both in real life, from Mary Wollstonecraft's failed attempt in 1795 to Virginia Woolf's successful one in 1941, and in fiction, from the Jailer's Daughter (another failed attempt) in Fletcher's and Shakespeare's *The Two Noble Kinsmen* in 1614 to Edna Pontellier in Kate Chopin's *The Awakening* (1899) and beyond.

In his identification of the 'Ophelia complex' Gaston Bachelard discussed the symbolic connections between women, water, and death, seeing drowning as an appropriate merging into the female element for women who are always associated with liquids: blood, milk, tears, and amniotic fluid. Moreover, as Elaine Showalter has demonstrated, the particular circumstances of Ophelia's madness have made her 'a potent and obsessive figure in our cultural mythology': she represents a powerful archetype in which female insanity and female sexuality are inextricably intertwined. Men may go mad for a number of reasons, including mental and spiritual stress, but women's madness is relentlessly associated with their bodies and their erotic desires. As Showalter notes, melancholy was a fashionable disease (or attitude) among young men in London from about 1580, but it was associated with intellectual and imaginative genius in them, whereas 'women's melancholy was seen instead as biological and emotional in its origins' ('Representing Ophelia' in Parker and Hartman, eds., *Shakespeare and the Question of Theory*, 1985, p. 81). The very word 'hysteria' implies a female, physiological condition, originating as it does from Greek 'hystera' meaning womb. King Lear, fighting off his own impending madness, equates '*Hysterica passio*' with the medical condition involving feelings of suffocation and giddiness known as 'the mother' (II. iv. 56–7). (See also Juliana Schiesari, *The Gendering of Melancholia*, 1992.)

On stage and in critical reception, Showalter argues that 'the representation of Ophelia changes independently of theories of the meaning of the play or the Prince, for it depends on attitudes towards women and madness' (pp. 91–2). She traces how stereotypes of female insanity affected the staging of the mad scene (IV. v), from sentimentalized Augustan versions through intense Romanticism to Pre-Raphaelite wistfulness. Post-Freudian Ophelias have signalled an incestuous interest in Polonius or Laertes, while the most recent performers have indicated schizophrenia, either as a serious mental illness or (in a feminist appropriation of the work of R. D. Laing) as an intelligible response to the experience of invalidation or the double bind within the family network.

When the well-known American feminist Carolyn Heilbrun reprinted her essay on 'Hamlet's Mother' in 1990 and used it as the lead piece in her book *Hamlet's Mother and Other Women*, she noted that when she first published it in 1957 she was 'a feminist critic waiting for a cause to join'. Her basic line in the essay was that critics and readers of the play have been too ready to accept Hamlet's view of Gertrude without questioning whether the overall view taken by the play (or its author) might be different. Many have joined the cause since 1975, the publication date of Juliet Dusinberre's *Shakespeare and the Nature of Women*, the first full-length feminist study of Shakespeare, and the date selected by Philip C. Kolin as the starting point for his annotated bibliography of *Shakespeare and Feminist Criticism* which lists forty-four items relating to *Hamlet* published between 1975 and his cut-off point in 1988. (More have of course appeared since.) This total is lower than those for *The Merchant of Venice* (forty-eight), *As You Like It* (fifty), *The Winter's Tale* (fifty-eight) and *Othello* (sixty-nine), and only just ahead of *The Taming of the Shrew* (forty-three), testifying to the prominence given to comedy in this period of feminist criticism, and the dominance of *Othello* amongst the tragedies. (*King Lear* gets thirty-eight items, *Antony and Cleopatra* thirty-four, and *Macbeth* thirty-three.)

Most of the items on *Hamlet* in these first thirteen years of feminist criticism are studies of the female characters – of Gertrude as a rare and problematic example of a Shakespearian mother, and of Ophelia as a victim, weak and silenced. This last adjective is perhaps surprising, given the extent to which her discovery of a voice in her madness causes the other characters considerable stress and embarrassment, but the obscenity and sexual innuendo in Ophelia's songs has still not been properly addressed by feminist critics although they are surely not as worried by it as nineteenth-century readers who felt the need to invent rustic wet-nurses for Ophelia's childhood (like the Nurse in *Romeo and Juliet*) to account for her knowledge of such things.

Some more general essays discuss the larger issues of femininity and masculinity in the play, covering such areas as the supposed effeminacy of Hamlet himself and the desire for male bonding, especially in Hamlet's relationship with Horatio. Many of the authors (especially those from North America) could be described as psychoanalytic critics as well as feminist critics and they are concerned to investigate the overlapping territories of language, fantasy, and sexuality. This emphasis has continued in post-1988 writing, though, as will be apparent in this and other chapters of this book, recent feminist critics have also been concerned with questions of history and staging.

Given that the majority of students of literature today are female as well as an increasing number of their teachers, it is probably the case that feminist critics have been responsible for the re-ordering of the canon, whereby a play like *Hamlet* with its relatively simplistic views of women as angels or whores becomes less interesting as a text to teach and/or write about. We are perhaps more critical of crude gender stereotypes, and while this can make for more interesting performances by actors who can allow Hamlet to be sensitive as well as virile without making the two mutually exclusive, students today (male as well as female) find it more difficult to empathize with a hero who seems so casual in his cruelty to the women in his life.

On a more positive note, the present critical climate may offer more scope for investigation of the phenomenon whereby Hamlet has been seen as effeminate in the past partly because he was seen as an intellectual: for a man to be intellectual was to be womanish, while at the same time it certainly did not follow that actual women were seen as intellectual, or that intellectual women were seen as anything other than unnatural. It should be possible for modern feminist critics to reassess at least this aspect of gender stereotyping in a more positive way as they both analyse and contribute to the extraordinarily rich afterlife of the play.

6

The Afterlife of *Hamlet*

There is no stable entity called *Hamlet*. The play which the printers of the 1603 Quarto boasted had been acted by the King's Men not only in the City of London but also 'in the two Universities of Cambridge and Oxford, and else-where' was quite unlike the text of *Hamlet* which we study today at school or university. It was not only much shorter, but many of the speeches are quite unrecognizable. Furthermore, the productions we see in the theatre usually differ, sometimes considerably, from the printed versions we buy in bookshops. And all of these, in their turn, differ from the film versions we watch in the cinema or on television.

One reason is the fact, already discussed in chapter 2, that there are three early texts of the play, each with a claim to authenticity, and all editions and all performances of *Hamlet* draw on these texts in different proportions.

Another reason is that actors and directors, for whose customers value for money includes going home at a reasonable hour, want their *Hamlet* fairly short. But scholarly editors, whose customers have all the time in the world and want a different kind of value for money, tend to print as much *Hamlet* as possible. This tension informs both the literary history and the performance history of the play, and the result has been an unstable literary text, an unstable performance text, and a fascinating interaction between the two.

In the (typically literary) interests of constructing the fullest possible text, some editors have expanded what they would regard as the reading text by drawing on what they would regard as the performance text. Thus, when he came to *Hamlet* in his 1709 edition of Shakespeare's works, Nicholas Rowe broke with his normal practice of just using the latest version of the Folio as his copy-text and incorporated some additional passages which were currently being performed on the London stage.

On the other hand, just as some editors feel they should be paying attention to what the actors are getting up to, so some actors and directors feel they should bring their texts in line with the reading texts authorized by Shakespeare's editors. David Garrick was notable for his radical alterations of the text, but he also began the process of consciously restoring lines – a process which was later to win J. P. Kemble praise for 'scholarship' and Macready a reputation for restoring the 'true text'. Indeed, from the eighteenth century onwards, the growth of the cult of Shakespeare the genius, combined with the growth of the profession of the scientific textual scholar, together encouraged actors to try to 'go back' to Shakespeare's 'original text'.

This impulse persists to the present day. But what is the original text? For Frank Benson at Stratford in 1899 and for Peter Hall at the Old Vic in 1975, both of whom were prepared to risk the commercial dangers of staging very long performances, this meant a conflation of every word they reckoned Shakespeare had written. Benson's amalgam of Q2 and F1 began in the afternoon and ended late in the evening, with a break for dinner. For others it has meant ignoring Q2 and F1 altogether and staging the short (normally disparaged) First Quarto – William Poel staged it in 1881 (see plate 6) and 1900, Donald Wolfit acted it in London's Arts Theatre Club in 1933, Sam Walters directed it at the Orange Tree Theatre in Richmond in 1985, and Dick McCaw's Medieval Players toured it round England in 1992.

While editors have been unable to agree upon the definitive state of the printed text, actors and directors have added to the multiplicity of *Hamlets* by cutting and rearranging that text. Hence, the play as performed is even less of a constant entity than the play as printed.

The version being performed in the late seventeenth century and throughout most of the eighteenth century was short by modern-day standards. In 1676, Shakespeare's godson William Davenant published his so-called 'Players Quarto' and informed his readers that 'This play being too long to be conveniently Acted, such places as might be least prejudicial to the Plot or Sense are left out upon the Stage'. The resulting text lacks many features to which twentieth-century students are used. Not only is the language 'refined', but Hamlet's advice to the Players, Polonius's advice to Laertes and most of Laertes' advice to Ophelia are missing. Of the famous longer speeches only 'To be or not to be' survives in its entirety. Some characters are simply cut (Voltemand, Cornelius and Reynaldo), while Fortinbras appears for the first time in the play's final scene. In 1732, Robert Wilks went further and cut Fortinbras entirely. This alteration became an accepted version of the play's ending and persisted in the theatre until 1897, when Fortinbras was reintroduced. Thus, for 165 years, audiences believed that the play ended with Hamlet's death. That the tradition still persisted into the twentieth century is recorded in the films made by Laurence Olivier (1948) and Tony Richardson (1969) – and even in some recent stage productions (for instance, the 1994 Birmingham Repertory Theatre production, directed by the American film-actor Richard Dreyfus).

The effect of cutting and rearranging a text is inevitably that the meaning of the text is altered. The Hamlet of the post-Restoration stage was less self-reproaching, and therefore seemingly more decisive as a revenger, than the one we have been trained, by exposure to fuller texts and post-Romantic interpretations, to expect. But cutting and rearranging are not the only ways in which actors and directors give meanings to *Hamlet* and thereby create new *Hamlets*. Whatever the words in the text which is chosen, there are always endless new ways of realizing that text on the stage or the screen.

This truth becomes evident as soon as we examine as simple a characteristic as Hamlet's visual appearance. Consider the conventional ad-man's image of Hamlet, a slim young man, clean-shaven, pale-faced, dressed in black and holding a skull. Nothing in this description, apart from his relative youth and his male gender, derives from any of the early texts. Indeed, both Q2 and F1 refer to Hamlet as being fat and bearded, and Richard Burbage, who was probably the first actor to play the part, seems to have been both. Subsequent Hamlets have included plenty of beards (in this century, for example, Nicol Williamson, Albert Finney, Derek Jacobi, Anton Lesser, and Mel Gibson), while Burbage's immediate successor Thomas Betterton, not only tended to corpulence but also, as we have said, put some strain on an audience's belief in Hamlet's youth, by going on acting the part until he was 74.

Even an established elementary gesture such as Hamlet's leap into Ophelia's grave derives not from the printed texts normally afforded authority by scholars (Q2 and F1) but from performance tradition. It is found in Q1, which most scholars regard as a reconstruction from a performance, and it seems to be described in an elegy written in 1619 to the recently dead Burbage:

> Oft have I seen him leap into the grave,
> Suiting the person which he seemed to have
> Of a sad lover with so true an eye
> That there, I would have sworn, he meant to die.

Fifteen years earlier, the poet Anthony Skoloker was probably recalling Burbage in the part, when he wrote that 'mad Hamlet puts off his cloathes, his shirt he only weares'. This reminds us that the portrayal of madness, frequently in grotesque terms, was a popular motif on the Elizabethan stage. Modern directors have often devoted much detailed attention to Ophelia's madness and required the actress to behave in an exaggeratedly distorted manner (notably Kathryn Pogson for Jonathan Miller in 1982 and Pernilla Ostergen for Ingmar Bergman in 1987), but they rarely require Hamlet to behave similarly. Ophelia's description of her dishevelled knock-kneed lover with his doublet all unbraced is rarely mirrored in his stage appearance. Just occasionally, however, a Hamlet follows Skoloker's description, and at least two modern productions have gone further: both Alan Howard for the Royal Shakespeare Company in 1970 and Stephen Dillane for Peter Hall in 1994 removed all their clothes and ran round the stage naked.

It is unlikely that many actors read up and consciously repeat what great actors of the past have done with the play. But there is plenty of evidence that actors copy features of performances they have seen for themselves. In the early nineteenth century, Edmund Kean's way of delivering certain lines was regarded as so affecting that generations of actors after him did them the same way. For example, as he moved to the wings having shouted to Ophelia, 'To a nunnery, go', he stopped, turned, walked back, took her hand tenderly, and kissed it. In the play scene, he would crawl across the stage from Ophelia's feet to Claudius's throne (see Plate 2). Kemble was criticized for repeating the Kean crawl when he took the play to Paris in 1827, and the Danish actress Asta Nielsen was still doing it when she played Hamlet in the German film-version of 1920.

The discussion so far has come to concentrate on Hamlet more than on *Hamlet*. This reflects the dominant pattern of the play's afterlife, which has been to isolate one character and concentrate obsessively on that character's character. John A. Mills has described the shift in taste which occurred when the brilliant David Garrick started playing Hamlet in 1742: 'Whereas Betterton, shaped for the most part by a Neoclassic aesthetic, had treated the character of Hamlet simply as one element in the overall design of the work, a design whose organising principle was action, or plot, Garrick operated within a newly emerging Romantic aesthetic, according to which the all-important factor, the cardinal principle of artistic cohesion, was the moment-to-moment psychological response of the protagonist to his fluid situation' (Mills, *Hamlet on Stage*, 1985, p. 33). This interest in Hamlet's psyche was taken up by Kean and became the dominant nineteenth- and twentieth-century approach to acting the role, reaching its apogee perhaps in Tyrone Guthrie's production of 1937, when he required his Hamlet to prepare for the role by consulting Ernest Jones, a psychoanalyst who had published an explanation of Hamlet's attitudes to his uncle, mother, and father cast in terms of Freud's theory of the Oedipus Complex.

Both film and television have the capacity to present actors in close-up, and television in particular deals largely in 'mug-shots'. The effect is inevitably to concentrate on the individual at the expense of the group, and to appear to be engaged in the minute revelation of psychological events. Hamlet as a character is an open invitation to such an approach – despite a film director's commitment to reaction shots, 49 per cent of the shots in Tony Richardson's 1969 film were of his Hamlet, Nicol Williamson, and 96 per cent of all the film's shots were in close-up. Radio and audiotape provide an aural equivalent of virtually continuous close-up, and Olivier's use of voice-over in his 1948 film for most of Hamlet's soliloquies reinforced the suggested intimacy with the Prince's interior life.

As well as shaping the play so that it concentrated on the tragedy of the main character (the tradition which culminates in A. C. Bradley's late-Victorian discussion of Shakespearian tragedy as an expression of the heroic element in human nature), the early actor-managers worked to ennoble that character. By 1772 Garrick was omitting everything that might tarnish Hamlet's image – even the voyage to England, because of the unattractive fact that he was prepared to send his old school-friends to their deaths. The wish to cleanse, hero-worship, and even sanctify Hamlet has surfaced in countless productions of the play, as in much of what has been written about him, ever since: it is particularly noticeable in the 1964 Russian film directed by Grigori Kozintsev. But it is sometimes counteracted by a wish to emphasize what some directors have regarded as Hamlet's less noble qualities, his indecision, his egotism, his insensitivity.

Part of Garrick's 1772 project was to make of the play a work of art which he could regard as great in terms of the aesthetic of his age. This meant reorganizing the plot so that it was more decorous, elevating the natures of many of the characters in the process. Thus, not only was the gravediggers' comic dialogue dropped in order to make the play more purely 'tragic', but Laertes was relieved of the blemish of having poisoned his sword, while Claudius, who no longer poisoned the drink and therefore his wife (she died offstage from insanity brought on by guilt), died trying to stop the duel between Laertes and Hamlet. Hamlet ran on Laertes' sword, and Horatio, having been dissuaded from killing Laertes in revenge, was finally persuaded to join him in ruling Denmark.

After Garrick, the next great Shakespearian actor was John Philip Kemble (1757–1853), strikingly handsome but (because asthmatic) slow-moving, slow-speaking, solemn and stiff. Hazlitt wrote that the distinguishing excellence of Kemble's acting may be summed up in one word – *intensity*, 'in seizing upon one feeling or idea, in insisting upon it, in never letting it go, and in working it up with a certain graceful consistency, and conscious grandeur of conception, to a very high degree of pathos or sublimity' (quoted in Mills, p.68). In the case of Hamlet, Kemble's one idea was melancholy. We find in this approach not only a reflection of the Romantic emphasis on feeling, but also a precursor of the modern desire to find a unifying concept to explain a play, a character and, above all, Hamlet.

But the preoccupation with Hamlet's character is not the only significant feature of the play's afterlife in performance. The

Tragicall Historie of Hamlet has a historical dimension, as much as it has a tragic dimension. Its presentation of the fall of a court, a ruling family, and a nation, raises the question of when and where this fall is supposed to take place. The wooden O of the Elizabethan stage was a demarcated *space*, a space to be filled by the imagination. In Shakespeare's treatment, the old story of Hamlet has found a local habitation (Elsinore), but there are few clues as to the period of history in which the events occur. We can therefore allocate them to the world of 'the past', or the world of 'abroad' if we want to, but the opportunity is also there to find in Elsinore the world of 'home' and 'today'.

In 1660 Davenant made a change to the performing conditions of plays which affected the whole subsequent history of theatre. Converting a tennis court in Lincoln's Inn Fields into his company's acting space, he transformed the nature of the audience's expectations by placing behind the Elizabethan stage a proscenium arch through which moveable painted scenery could be seen. The actors thereby became elements in an aesthetic composition within a picture frame; at the same time the characters they played became defined as belonging to a particular place and time.

Pepys wrote with pleasure of the novelty of seeing *Hamlet* 'done with scenes'. It was the first of Shakespeare's plays to be presented with perspective scenery. Two hundred years later the play was not only being 'done with scenes' but entirely subservient to the tyranny of 'scenes', so that it became a series of iconic moments: Macready wanted his Shakespeare 'fitly illustrated' as 'a series of glorious pictures'. But on the whole, Victorian directors and designers used their lavish scenery to focus attention on the star actor. By contrast, Gordon Craig's famous set for Stanislavsky's Moscow Arts Theatre production of 1912 reduced the actors to puppets, dwarfed by the monumental sets towering over them. As it happens, both approaches make sense of *Hamlet*, which has been variously interpreted as exploring in depth the unique nature of its hero and, on the other hand, describing the overwhelming forces – psychological, political, metaphysical – which conspire against him. But this whole process of definition through physical and temporal contextualization not only reflects the power of the director and, very often too, the designer; it also reflects the desire of first actor-managers and then directors to impose meaning on the play.

The developing science of archaeology and the fashion for historical fiction encouraged nineteenth-century actor-managers to go for historical accuracy in the visual staging of the plays. Kean spent a great deal of money recreating the castle of Elsinore, and Fechter broke with tradition by dressing Hamlet in Viking gear rather than in the velvet and lace of an English aristocrat. The reaction when it came was also archaeological in inspiration. This time, the project was to rediscover the conditions of Elizabethan staging. In the 1880s William Poel rejected picture sets by reinventing bare staging, and Barry Jackson claimed to be 'getting back to Garrick' and to Shakespeare's own practices when his director at the Birmingham Repertory Theatre, H. K. Ayliff, mounted a modern-dress production at London's Kingsway Theatre in 1925. Ayliff rejected the dominant Romantic tone of Victorian Shakespeare, picking up instead the mood of his own age: Ivor Brown called Colin Keith-Johnston's Hamlet 'a loose-tongued, bawdy-minded, and savage product of youthful disenchantment' (see Plate 7). Forty years on, B. A. Young found in David Warner's Hamlet at Stratford-upon-Avon the embodiment of rebellious youth in the age of the Bomb, describing him as a 'beatnik'.

Once modern dress had become accepted (as in Tyrone Guthrie's 1938 production, with its memorable funeral scene with mackintoshes and dripping umbrellas), it opened up three further possibilities for designers. They could set the play in other periods too, as when Michael Benthall directed a Victorian *Hamlet* at Stratford in 1948. They could set the play in the theatre itself, as when John Gielgud directed Richard Burton in New York in 1964 and the set was a simulated rehearsal room. Finally, they could set the play in no realistic place or period at all, as when Hans Gratzer's 1979 Viennese production had Hamlet delivering 'To be or not to be' while hanging over the audience from a horizontal bar.

The chief characteristic of *Hamlet*'s afterlife is its universal fame. The German physicist Werner Heisenberg recalled visiting Kronberg Castle in 1924 with Niels Bohr, who said

Isn't it strange how this castle changes as soon as one imagines that Hamlet lived here? As scientists we believe that a castle consists only of stones, and admire the way the architect put them together. The stones, the green roof with its patina, the wood carvings in the church, constitute the whole castle. None of this should be changed by the fact that Hamlet lived here, and yet it is changed completely. Suddenly the walls and the ramparts speak a different language. The courtyard becomes an entire world, a dark corner reminds us of the darkness in the human soul, we hear Hamlet's 'To be or not to be' (quoted in Gordon Mills, *Hamlet's Castle: the Study of Literature as Social Experience*, Austin, Texas, 1976, p. 51).

Hamlet came to be known outside Britain midway through the eighteenth century. Starting in France, where it was first translated in 1745, it reached Russia in 1748 and America in 1759. Within a hundred years it had not only spread to most of the rest of the world, but foreign actors were visiting London to perform the play to English audiences. While some failed to impress – an Indian company in 1877 had to sell all their stage equipment to raise the price of their fares home – others had great success. The theatrical style in which Hamlets deliver their lines was probably changed for ever in 1861 when the Frenchman, Charles Fechter, despite some misunderstanding of Shakespeare's language, intro-duced to the part a naturalism he had learnt while creating the part of Armand Duval in *La Dame aux Camélias.*

Meanwhile, new territories were being conquered. By the 1870s, despite the unfortunate fact that their language lacked the verb 'to be', *Hamlet* was appearing in Japanese: by 1960 it was sufficiently assimilated into Japanese culture to have inspired at least five novels and Kurosawa's film.

As well as continually varying its dramatic shape and taking on new meanings, and as well as being read and performed in more and more corners of the world, Shakespeare's play and the ideas which have been discovered within it have found their way into any number of other cultural forms. There have been at least fifty films since Sarah Bernhardt recorded the duel scene in Paris in 1900. Stoppard's *Rosencrantz and Guildenstern are Dead* is by no means the only work of art to play a variation on Shakespeare's treatment of material in the play: Iris Murdoch's *The Black Prince* (1973) and Alan Isler's *The Prince of West End Avenue* (1994) are just two *Hamlet*-novels in English. 'Hamletism' became an intellectual concept in nineteenth-century Russia. Chekhov quotes the play in *The Cherry Orchard* and in part constructs the plot of *The Seagull* around Hamlet's relationship with Gertrude. Liszt was inspired to compose a symphonic poem, Domenico Scarlatti and Ambroise Thomas composed operas. When Harriet Smithson played Ophelia in Paris in 1827, a cult of Ophelia was born. Delacroix produced lithographs of her (see Plate 3), Victor Hugo and Arthur Rimbaud wrote under her influence, and Hector Berlioz composed *La Mort d'Ophelie.*

And what generated its fame was *Hamlet*'s infinite capacity to generate meanings, private and public, personal and political. Of these it is the category of the political which has been the most potent in the second half of the twentieth century.

Hamlet believes that 'Denmark's a prison' and its leader a corrupt and corrupting criminal. Those throughout the world who have felt alienated and oppressed by the regimes under which they have been forced to live have seized on *Hamlet* for enlightenment and reassurance. It was performed before enthusiastic audiences in Broadmoor Prison in 1989. It was performed in the Moscow Maly Theatre in 1837, when Pavel Mochalov's portrayal of Hamlet was greeted rapturously as a defiant cry for freedom and justice: Belinsky wrote 'Hamlet! . . . Do you grasp the meaning of this word? . . . it is you, it is I, it is every one of us!' Where the play's presentation of an oppressive regime once provided an outlet for feeling against the tsars, it later provided an outlet for feeling against Stalin (who banned the play) and the tyranny of communism. Kozintsev's 1964 film, whose Hamlet was not only presented as a political and spiritual hero but played by an actor well known for having been imprisoned by both the Germans and then the Russian authorities, used a version of the text prepared by Boris Pasternak; Yuri Lyubimov's 1971 production in the Taganka Theatre in Moscow began with Hamlet reciting 'Hamlet', Pasternak's poem in his banned novel *Dr Zhivago.* This production, which was restaged with a British cast at the Leicester Haymarket in 1989, was dominated by an enormous curtain which swung across the stage to reveal and conceal ever-present eavesdroppers (see Plate 8).

Nor was the USSR the only section of that huge stage behind the Iron Curtain where directors and audiences in the second half of the twentieth century turned to *Hamlet* and put themselves at risk by using Shakespeare's tragedy to hint at what they regarded as the tragedies of their own countries – Poland, Romania, Bulgaria. In East Germany, according to Maik Hamburger, they could get away with it because 'the theatre was on the one hand respected by the authorities as a pillar of cultural prestigiousness, on the other hand it was the genre least harassed by them because of its ephemeral nature and its relative insignificance vis-à-vis the printed word or the mass media' (*Shakespeare Survey 48*, 1995, p. 171). But *Hamlet*'s potential political significances are multiple, sometimes conflictual. W. Rohan Quince has written an account of its political afterlife in South Africa, where it was first played in Port Elizabeth as early as 1799. Since then, performances have been used 'by English-speaking whites to maintain the position of cultural superiority, by Afrikaners to challenge this position and to validate Afrikaner culture, and by Coloureds, Indians, and blacks to establish their bid for inclusion in the rights and privileges of an equal society' ('*Hamlet* on the South African Stage', 1988).

7

Conclusion

We could simply leave *Hamlet* in the newly egalitarian South Africa, where the play and its hero will no doubt continue to be reread and reappropriated by all sections of a multi-ethnic and multi-cultural society. The precise origins of Shakespeare's play are difficult to determine – when precisely did he write it? when did he revise it and why? – but it has already had an extra-ordinarily rich past and seems set for a long and varied future.

In the last year alone, performances we have ourselves had the opportunity to attend have included one by an all-female cast at the University of Warwick, one by a mixed-race cast with an Asian Hamlet at the University of Wales, Cardiff, and one by prisoners and staff with a black Hamlet at Brixton prison in London. These were in addition to several professional productions in London (including one in the open air), a ballet, a puppet version, and film versions from five different countries (Germany, Italy, Japan, the UK, and the USA).

Also in the last year, we have watched a television programme on *Playing the Dane* and a cinema programme of film and video parodies of 'To be or not to be'; we have attended academic conferences and delivered papers on *Hamlet* in London, Stratford, Oxford, Cambridge, Sheffield, Sofia, Barcelona, New York, Hawaii, and Osaka; we have tried in our classrooms to introduce a new generation of students to *Hamlet*; we have failed to keep up with all the editions, translations, books, and articles pouring from the world's presses. For a play whose status is apparently not what it was, *Hamlet* is not doing too badly as it approaches the 400th anniversary of its first performance. We wish it well, and feel honoured to be able to contribute to the ongoing tradition of reception and analysis through this short book.

1. Hamlet and the Ghost of his Father. Design for Charles Fechter's 1864 production

2. Hamlet and the Court watch 'The Murder of Gonzago'. 1842 painting by Daniel Maclise

3. The Death of Ophelia. 1843 lithograph by Eugène Delacroix

4. Amblett. One of the earliest pictures of the pre-Shakespearian hero

5. Asta Nielsen as Hamlet. Publicity still for the 1920 film

6. Court Scene from William Poel's 1881 production on an Elizabethan stage at St George's Hall

7. The Funeral of Ophelia. From H. K. Ayliff's 1925 production at the Kingsway Theatre

8. Hamlet watches Claudius attempting to pray. From Yuri Lyubimov's 1989 production at the Leicester Haymarket Theatre

Select Bibliography

EDITIONS OF *Hamlet*

Variorum, ed. Horace Howard Furness, 2 vols. (Philadelphia, 1877).
New Penguin, ed. T. J. B. Spencer (Harmondsworth, 1980).
New Arden (Arden 2), ed. Harold Jenkins (London, 1982).
New Cambridge, ed. Philip Edwards (Cambridge, 1985).
Oxford, ed. G. R. Hibbard (Oxford, 1987).
Shakespearean Originals (First Quarto), ed. Graham Holderness and Bryan Loughrey (Hemel Hempstead, 1992).

CRITICAL WORKS

Adelman, Janet, *Suffocating Mothers: Fantasies of Maternal Origin in Shakespeare's Plays, 'Hamlet' to 'The Tempest'* (London, 1992). A psychoanalytic study of Shakespeare's confrontation of maternal power in *Hamlet* and other plays.

Bloom, Harold (ed.), *Major Literary Characters: Hamlet* (New York, 1990). For relevant extracts from Johann Wolfgang von Goethe, A. C. Bradley, Sigmund Freud, T. S. Eliot, Ernest Jones.

Bullough, Geoffrey, *Narrative and Dramatic Sources of Shakespeare*, vol. 7 (London, 1973). For some of the source material.

Charney, Maurice (ed.), *'Bad' Shakespeare: Revaluations of the Shakespeare Canon* (Rutherford, New Jersey, 1988). Relevant material in Charney's Introduction (pp. 9–18) and in Alex Newell's 'The Etiology of Horatio's Inconsistencies' (pp. 143–56).

Clayton, Thomas (ed.), *The 'Hamlet' First Published (Q1, 1603): Origins, Form, Intertextualities* (Newark, 1992). A collection of essays on Q1.

Codden, Karin S., ' "Such Strange Desygns": Madness, Subjectivity, and Treason in *Hamlet* and Elizabethan Culture', *Renaissance Drama* XX (1989), 51–75. A topical reading of the play with reference to the decline of the Earl of Essex.

Donawerth, Jane, *Shakespeare and the Sixteenth-Century Study of Language* (Urbana, Illinois, 1984). The chapter on *Hamlet* is a discussion of Shakespeare's self-conscious use of Renaissance ideas about language in this play.

Dusinberre, Juliet, *Shakespeare and the Nature of Women* (London, 1975, 1995). The first full-length feminist study of Shakespeare, reissued with a new Preface in 1995.

Edmonds, Jill, 'Princess Hamlet', in Viv Gardner and Susan Rutherford (eds.), *The New Woman and Her Sisters: Feminism and Theatre 1850–1914* (Hemel Hempstead, 1992), 59–76. A selective survey of female performers of Hamlet.

Elam, Keir, *The Semiotics of Theatre and Drama* (London, 1980). A deployment of techniques from semiotics and linguistics in an analysis of the opening of the play through a form of dramatic notation.

Eliot, T. S., 'Hamlet' (1919), in *Selected Essays* (London, 1951). Famous for describing *Hamlet* as 'an artistic failure' because of Shakespeare's difficulty in finding an 'objective correlative' for the emotions evoked.

Foakes, R. A., *'Hamlet' versus 'Lear'* (Cambridge, 1993). An analysis of the reception of the two plays, a brief discussion of *Hamlet*'s early textual history, and a critique of modern readings.

Hamburger, Maik, 'Are You a Party in this Business? Consolidation and Subversion in East German Shakespeare Productions', *Shakespeare Survey 48* (Cambridge, 1995), 171–84.

Hansen, William F., *Saxo Grammaticus and the Life of Hamlet* (Nebraska, 1983). Traces the legend and presents Saxo's version in his *History of the Danes* in full.

Hattaway, Michael, *'Hamlet': The Critics' Debate* (London, 1987). A succinct survey of the plurality of critical approaches.

Kolin, Philip C., *Shakespeare and Feminist Criticism: An Annotated Bibliography and Commentary* (New York, 1991). Covers 439 books and essays from 1975 to 1988.

Kurland, Stuart M., *'Hamlet* and the Scottish Succession', *Studies in English Literature*, 34 (1994), 279–300. A topical reading of the play with reference to anxieties about the succession and the fear of foreign intervention.

Maher, Mary Z., *Modern Hamlets and their Soliloquies* (Iowa City, Iowa, 1992). Considers a selection of interpretations from John Gielgud (1929) to Kevin Kline (1990).

Mahood, M. M., *Shakespeare's Wordplay* (London, 1957). Particularly good on the puns.

McDonald, Russ (ed.), *Shakespeare Reread* (New York, 1994). Several contributors use readings of *Hamlet* to exemplify modern approaches to 'close reading'.

Mills, John A., *Hamlet on Stage: the Great Tradition* (Connecticut, 1985). A detailed survey of famous performances from Richard Burbage (1603?) to Albert Finney (1976).

O'Brien, Ellen J., 'Revision by Excision: Rewriting Gertrude', in *Shakespeare Survey 45* (1992), 27–35. A survey of the cutting of the role on stage from 1755 to 1900.

Parker, Patricia, *Literary Fat Ladies: Rhetoric, Gender, Property* (London, 1987). An analysis of the links between rhetoric and gender in *Hamlet* and other literary texts.

Parker, Patricia, '*Othello* and *Hamlet*: Dilation, Spying, and the "Secret Place" of Woman', in Russ McDonald (ed.), *Shakespeare Reread* (New York, 1994), 105–46. A reading of both plays with reference to the growth of a secret service and a quasi-pornographic gynaecology.

Patterson, Annabel, ' "The Very Age and Body of the Time His Form and Pressure": Rehistoricizing Shakespeare's Theater', *New Literary History*, 20 (1988–9), 83–104. A critique of some new historicist readings.

Prosser, Eleanor, *Hamlet and Revenge* (London, 1967). Discusses the Elizabethan revenge play and its ethics.

Quince, W. Rohan, '*Hamlet* on the South African Stage', *Hamlet Studies*, 10, 1988, 144–51. Discusses productions from 1799 to 1982.

Rose, Jacqueline, 'Sexuality in the Reading of Shakespeare: *Hamlet* and *Measure for Measure*', in John Drakakis (ed.), *Alternative Shakespeares* (London, 1985), 95–118. An examination of sexuality (sexism) in classic readings of *Hamlet* by T. S. Eliot, Ernest Jones, and others.

Schiesari, Juliana, *The Gendering of Melancholia* (New York and London, 1992). Includes discussion of Hamlet's madness and Ophelia's madness in relation to the positive valorizing of masculine melancholy and the relative devalorizing of feminine melancholy.

Scofield, Martin, *The Ghosts of Hamlet: the Play and Modern Writers* (Cambridge, 1980). The first half of this book explores the presence of *Hamlet* as an influence in the work of a range of authors, from Mallarmé to Kafka.

Shakespeare Survey 45: 'Hamlet' and its Afterlife (Cambridge, 1992). Special issue of the journal containing seven essays on this topic.

Showalter, Elaine, 'Representing Ophelia: Women, Madness, and the Responsibilities of Feminist Criticism', in Patricia Parker and Geoffrey Hartman (eds.), *Shakespeare and the Question of Theory* (London, 1985), 77–94. An account of the representation of Ophelia in painting, photography, psychiatry, and literature as well as on stage.

Taylor, Gary, *Reinventing Shakespeare: a Cultural History from the Restoration to the Present* (London, 1990). A very readable account of the ways in which Shakespeare has been repeatedly 'reinvented' over the last 350 years in order to suit the needs of his readers.

Taylor, Neil, 'The Films of *Hamlet*', in Anthony Davies and Stanley Wells (eds.), *Shakespeare and the Moving Image: the Plays on Film and Television* (Cambridge, 1994), 180–95). A brief study of the Olivier, Kozintsev, Richardson, Bennett, Zeffirelli and *Shakespeare: Animated Tales* film versions.

Tennenhouse, Leonard, 'Violence done to Women on the Renaissance Stage' in Nancy Armstrong and Leonard Tennenhouse (eds.), *The Violence of Representation* (London, 1989), 77–97. A new historicist reading of the sexual issues in terms of Elizabethan/Jacobean politics.

Thompson, Ann, and John O. Thompson, *Shakespeare, Meaning and Metaphor* (Brighton, 1987). One chapter discusses metaphors of the human body in *Hamlet* in relation to modern theories about metaphor and synecdoche.

Tillyard, E. M. W., *Shakespeare's Problem Plays* (London, 1950). *Hamlet* is categorized as 'problematic' in terms of the religious and psychological issues it raises.

Trousdale, Marion, *Shakespeare and the Rhetoricians* (London, 1982). Relates Renaissance views of rhetoric to Shakespeare's methods of dramatic composition.

Vickers, Brian, *The Artistry of Shakespeare's Prose* (London, 1968). Valuable study of Hamlet's wit in prose conversation.

Vining, Edward P., *The Mystery of Hamlet: An Attempt to Solve an Old Problem* (Philadelphia, 1881). An argument that Shakespeare, in revising his play, became increasingly interested in the possibility of Hamlet being a woman.

Wright, George T., 'Hendiadys and *Hamlet*', *Publications of the Modern Language Association*, 96 (1981), 168–93. Argues for the special importance of this figure in the play.

Index

Recent and
Forthcoming Titles
in the
New Series of

WRITERS AND
THEIR WORK

WRITERS AND THEIR WORK

RECENT & FORTHCOMING TITLES

Title	Author
Aphra Behn	Sue Wiseman
Angela Carter	Lorna Sage
Children's Literature	Kimberley Reynolds
John Clare	John Lucas
Joseph Conrad	Cedric Watts
John Donne	Stevie Davies
Henry Fielding	Jenny Uglow
Elizabeth Gaskell	Kate Flint
William Golding	Kevin McCarron
Hamlet	Ann Thompson & Neil Taylor
David Hare	Jeremy Ridgman
Tony Harrison	Joe Kelleher
William Hazlitt	J.B. Priestley; R.L. Brett (introduction by Michael Foot)
George Herbert	T.S. Eliot (introduction by Peter Porter)
Henry James - The Later Writing	Barbara Hardy
King Lear	Terence Hawkes
Doris Lessing	Elizabeth Maslen
David Lodge	Bernard Bergonzi
Christopher Marlowe	Thomas Healy
Andrew Marvell	Annabel Patterson
Ian McEwan	Kiernan Ryan
Walter Pater	Laurel Brake
Jean Rhys	Helen Carr
Dorothy Richardson	Carol Watts
The Sensation Novel	Lyn Pykett
Edmund Spenser	Colin Burrow
Leo Tolstoy	John Bayley
Charlotte Yonge	Alethea Hayter

TITLES IN PREPARATION

Title	Author
Peter Ackroyd	Susana Onega
Antony and Cleopatra	Ken Parker
W.H. Auden	Stan Smith
Jane Austen	Robert Clark
Elizabeth Bowen	Maud Ellmann
Emily Brontë	Stevie Davies
A.S. Byatt	Richard Todd
Lord Byron	J. Drummond Bone
Geoffrey Chaucer	Steve Ellis
Caryl Churchill	Elaine Aston
S.T. Coleridge	Stephen Bygrave
Charles Dickens	Rod Mengham

TITLES IN PREPARATION

Title	Author
George Eliot	*Josephine McDonagh*
E.M. Forster	*Nicholas Royle*
Brian Friel	*Geraldine Higgins*
Graham Greene	*Peter Mudford*
Thomas Hardy	*Peter Widdowson*
Seamus Heaney	*Andrew Murphy*
Henry IV	*Peter Bogdanov*
Henrik Ibsen	*Sally Ledger*
James Joyce	*Steven Connor*
Rudyard Kipling	*Jan Montefiore*
Franz Kafka	*Michael Wood*
John Keats	*Kelvin Everest*
Philip Larkin	*Laurence Lerner*
D.H. Lawrence	*Linda Ruth Williams*
A Midsummer Night's Dream	*Helen Hackett*
William Morris	*Anne Janowitz*
Brian Patten	*Linda Cookson*
Alexander Pope	*Pat Rogers*
Sylvia Plath	*Elizabeth Bronfen*
Richard II	*Margaret Healy*
Lord Rochester	*Peter Porter*
Romeo and Juliet	*Sasha Roberts*
Christina Rossetti	*Katherine Burlinson*
Salman Rushdie	*Damian Grant*
Stevie Smith	*Alison Light*
Sir Walter Scott	*John Sutherland*
Wole Soyinka	*Mpalive Msiska*
Jonathan Swift	*Claude Rawson*
The Tempest	*Gordon McMullan*
J.R.R. Tolkien	*Charles Moseley*
Mary Wollstonecraft	*Jane Moore*
Evelyn Waugh	*Malcolm Bradbury*
Angus Wilson	*Peter Conradi*
Virginia Woolf	*Laura Marcus*
William Wordsworth	*Nicholas Roe*
Working Class Fiction	*Ian Haywood*
W.B. Yeats	*Ed Larrissy*

RECENT & FORTHCOMING TITLES

DORIS LESSING
Elizabeth Maslen

Covering a wide range of Doris Lessing's works up to 1992, including all her novels and a selection of her short stories and non-fictional writing, this study demonstrates how Lessing's commitment to political and cultural issues and her explorations of inner space have remained unchanged throughout her career. Maslen also examines Lessing's writings in the context of the work of Bakhtin and Foucault, and of feminist theories.

Elizabeth Maslen is Senior Lecturer in English at Queen Mary and Westfield College, University of London.

0 7463 0705 5 paperback 80pp

JOSEPH CONRAD
Cedric Watts

This authoritative introduction to the range of Conrad's work draws out the distinctive thematic preoccupations and technical devices running through the main phases of the novelist's literary career. Watts explores Conrad's importance and influence as a moral, social and political commentator on his times and addresses recent controversial developments in the evaluation of this magisterial, vivid, complex and problematic author.

"...balanced insights into the controversies surrounding Conrad".
Times Educational Supplement.

Cedric Watts, Professor of English at the University of Sussex, is recognized internationally as a leading authority on the life and works of Joseph Conrad.

0 7463 0737 3 paperback 80pp

JOHN DONNE
Stevie Davies

Raising a feminist challenge to the body of male criticism which congratulates Donne on the 'virility' of his writing, Dr Davies' stimulating and accessible introduction to the full range of the poet's work sets it in the wider cultural, religious and political context conditioning the mind of this turbulent and brilliant poet. Davies also explores the profound emotionalism of Donne's verse and offers close, sensitive readings of individual poems.

Stevie Davies is a literary critic and novelist who has written on a wide range of literature.

0 7463 0738 1 paperback 96pp

THE SENSATION NOVEL
Lyn Pykett

A 'great fact' in the literature of its day, a 'disagreeable' sign of the times, or an ephemeral minor sub-genre? What was the sensation novel, and why did it briefly dominate the literary scene in the 1860s? This wide-ranging study analyses the broader significance of the sensation novel as well as looking at it in its specific cultural context.

Lyn Pykett is Senior Lecturer in English at the University of Wales in Aberystwyth.

0 7463 0725 X paperback 96pp

CHRISTOPHER MARLOWE
Thomas Healy

The first study for many years to explore the whole range of Marlowe's writing, this book uses recent ideas about the relation between literature and history, popular and élite culture, and the nature of Elizabethan theatre to reassess his significance. An ideal introduction to one of the most exciting and innovative of English writers, Thomas Healy's book provides fresh insights into all of Marlowe's important works.

Thomas Healy is Senior Lecturer in English at Birkbeck College, University of London.

0 7463 0707 1 paperback 96pp

ANDREW MARVELL
Annabel Patterson

This state-of-the art guide to one of the seventeenth century's most intriguing poets examines Marvell's complex personality and beliefs and provides a compelling new perspective on his work. Annabel Patterson – one of the leading Marvell scholars – provides comprehensive introductions to Marvell's different self-representations and places his most famous poems in their original context.

Annabel Patterson is Professor of English at Yale University and author of *Marvell and the Civic Crown* (1978).

0 7463 0715 2 paperback 96pp

WILLIAM GOLDING
Kevin McCarron

This comprehensive study takes an interdisciplinary approach to the work of William Golding, placing particular emphasis on the anthropological perspective missing from most other texts on his writings. The book covers all his novels, questioning the status of *Lord of the Flies* as his most important work, and giving particular prominence to *The Inheritors, Pincher Martin, The Spire* and The Sea Trilogy. This in-depth evaluation provides many new insights into the works of one of the twentieth century's greatest writers.

Kevin McCarron is Lecturer in English at Roehampton Institute, where he teaches Modern English and American Literature. He has written widely on the work of William Golding.

0 7463 0735 7 paperback 80pp

WALTER PATER
Laurel Brake

This is the only critical study devoted to the works of Pater, an active participant in the nineteenth-century literary marketplace as an academic, journalist, critic, writer of short stories and novelist. Approaching Pater's writings from the perspective of cultural history, this book covers all his key works, both fiction and non-fiction.

"...grounded in an unmatched scholarly command of Pater's life and writing."
English Association Newsletter

Laurel Brake is Lecturer in Literature at Birkbeck College, University of London, and has written widely on Victorian literature and in particular on Pater.

0 7463 0716 0 paperback 96pp

ANGELA CARTER
Lorna Sage

Angela Carter was probable the most inventive British novelist of her generation. In this fascinating study, Lorna Sage argues that one of the reasons for Carter's enormous success is the extraordinary intelligence with which she read the cultural signs of our times – from structuralism and the study of folk tales in the 1960s – to, more recently, fairy stories and gender politics. The book explores the roots of Carter's originality and covers all her novels, as well as some short stories and non-fiction.

"...this reappraisal of an interesting novelist explores the roots of her originality .. . a useful introduction to the work of Angela Carter.' **Sunday Telegraph**

Lorna Sage teaches at the University of East Anglia, where she is currently Dean of the School of English and American Studies.

0 7463 0727 6 paperback 96pp

IAN McEWAN
Kiernan Ryan

This is the first book-length study of one of the most original and exciting writers to have emerged in Britain in recent years. It provides an introduction to the whole range of McEwan's work, examining his novels, short stories and screenplays in depth and tracing his development from the 'succès de scandale' of *First Love, Last Rites* to the haunting vision of the acclaimed *Black Dogs*.

"(Written with)...conviction and elegance." **The Irish Times**

Kiernan Ryan is Fellow and Director of Studies in English at New Hall, University of Cambridge.

0 7463 0742 X paperback 80pp

ELIZABETH GASKELL
Kate Flint

Recent critical appraisal has focused on Gaskell both as a novelist of industrial England and on her awareness of the position of women and the problems of the woman writer. Kate Flint reveals how for Gaskell the condition of women was inseparable from broader issues of social change. She shows how recent modes of feminist criticism and theories of narrative work together to illuminate the radicalism and experimentalism which we find in Gaskell's fiction.

Kate Flint is University Lecturer in Victorian and Modern English Literature, and Fellow of Linacre College, Oxford.

0 7463 0718 7 paperback 96pp

KING LEAR
Terence Hawkes

In his concise but thorough analysis of *King Lear* Terence Hawkes offers a full and clear exposition of its complex narrative and thematic structure. By examining the play's central preoccupations and through close analysis of the texture of its verse he seeks to locate it firmly in its own history and the social context to which, clearly, it aims to speak. The result is a challenging critical work which both deepens understanding of this great play and illuminates recent approaches to it.

Terence Hawkes has written several books on both Shakespeare and modern critical theory. He is Professor of English at the University of Wales, Cardiff.

0 7463 0739 X paperback 96pp

JEAN RHYS
Helen Carr

Drawing on her own experience of alienation and conflict as a white-Creole woman, Rhys's novels are recognised as important explorations of gender and colonial power relations. Using feminist and post-colonial theory, Helen Carr's study places Rhys's work in relation to modernist and postmodernist writing and looks closely at how autobiographical material is used by the writer to construct a devastating critique of the greed and cruelty of patriarchy and the Empire.

Helen Carr is Lecturer in English at Goldsmiths College, University of London.

0 7463 0717 9 paperback 96pp

DOROTHY RICHARDSON
Carol Watts

Dorothy Richardson is a major modern novelist whose work is only now beginning to attract the attention of critics, feminists, and cultural theorists. She was one of the earliest novelists to consider the importance of developing a new aesthetic form to represent women's experience and in doing so, she explored many of the new art forms of the twentieth century. Carol Watt's book is an innovative study of her extraordinary thirteen-volume novel, *Pilgrimage* and offers an exciting challenge to the common readings of literary modernism.

Carol Watts is Lecturer in English Literature at Birkbeck College, University of London.

0 7463 0708 X paperback 112pp

APHRA BEHN
Sue Wiseman

Aphra Behn was prolific in all the most commercial genres of her time and wrote widely on many of the most controversial issues of her day – sexual and cultural difference, slavery, politics, and money. Bringing together an analysis of the full range of her writing in poetry, prose and drama, this is the first book-length critical study of Aphra Behn's work, much of which has been hitherto relatively neglected.

Sue Wiseman is Lecturer in English at the University of Warwick.

0 7463 0709 8 paperback 96pp

HENRY FIELDING
Jenny Uglow

In this fresh introduction to his work, Uglow looks at Fielding in his own historical context and in the light of recent critical debates. She identifies and clarifies many of Fielding's central ideas, such as those of judgement, benevolence and mercy which became themes in his novels. Looking not only at the novels, but also at Fielding's drama, essays, journalism and political writings, Uglow traces the author's development, clarifies his ideas on his craft, and provides a fascinating insight into eighteenth-century politics and society.

Jenny Uglow is a critic and publisher.

0 7463 0751 9 paperback 96pp

HENRY JAMES
The Later Writing
Barbara Hardy

Barbara Hardy focuses on Henry James's later works, dating from 1900 to 1916. Offering new readings of the major novels and a re-evaluation of the criticism to date, she considers language and theme in a number of Jamesian works, including *The Ambassadors, The Wings of the Dove* and *The Golden Bowl,* and engages with his autobiographical and travel writing and literary criticism. Hardy's analysis traces two dominant themes – the social construction of character and the nature of creative imagination – and reveals James to be a disturbing analyst of inner life.

Barbara Hardy is Professor Emeritus at Birkbeck College, University of London.

0 7463 0748 9 paperback 96pp

DAVID LODGE
Bernard Bergonzi

Internationally celebrated as both a novelist and a literary critic, David Lodge is one of Britain's most successful and influential living writers. He has been instrumental in introducing and explaining modern literary theory to British readers while maintaining, in regard to his own work, "faith in the future of realistic fiction". Bergonzi's up-to-date and comprehensive study covers both Lodge's critical writing as well as his novels of the past 35 years (from *The Picturegoers* to *Therapy*) and explores how he expresses and convincingly combines metafiction, realism, theology and dazzling comedy.

Bernard Bergonzi is Emeritus Professor of English at the University of Warwick.

0 7463 0755 1 paperback 80pp

DAVID HARE
Jeremy Ridgman

David Hare is one of the most prolific, challenging, and culturally acclaimed playwrights in Britain today. Jeremy Ridgman's study focuses on the dramatic method that drives the complex moral and political narratives of Hare's work. He considers its relationship to its staging and performance, looking in particular at the dramatist's collaborations with director, designer, and performer. Hare's writing for the theatre since 1970 is set alongside his work for television and film and his achievements as director and translator, to provide a detailed insight into key areas of his dramatic technique particularly dialogue, narrative, and epic form.

Jeremy Ridgman is Senior Lecturer in the Department of Drama and Theatre Studies at Roehampton Institute, London

0 7463 0774 8 paperback 96pp

TONY HARRISON
Joe Kelleher

Tony Harrison has been acclaimed worldwide, not only for his slim volumes of poetry but also for his lyric sequences and long poems, for his adaptations and original plays for the theatre, his opera libretti, and his verse films for television. Kelleher argues that Harrison's unique achievement is to ransack a whole range of traditions in order to carve out in verse, a very innovative and contemporary mode of public utterance.

Joe Kelleher is a playwright and Lecturer in Drama at Roehampton Institute.

0 7463 0789 6 paperback 96pp

CHARLOTTE YONGE
Alethea Hayter

Charlotte Yonge was a best-selling Victorian author and widely admired by her greatest literary contemporaries in the mid-ninteenth century but for the next hundred years, ignored or vilified by critics. Her work has only recently begun to receive the attention it deserves from biographers, historians and feminists. Alethea Hayter's appraisal of Yonge as a writer surveys the full range of her work – her non-fictional studies in history and wild-life, as well as her family chronicles, historical novels and children's books. Yonge emerges as a perceptive writer who well deserves the renewed interest in her and her work.

Alethea Hayter is a literary critic and historian, who has pubished a number of books on nineteenth-century literature.

0 7463 0781 0 paperback 96pp